Time to **Rejoice**

Devotions Celebrating God's Love

Patsy Clairmont
Mary Graham
Lisa Harper
Mandisa

Marilyn Meberg
Luci Swindoll
Sheila Walsh
Lisa Whelchel

Women of Faith

Thomas Nelson

Since 1798

NASHVILLE   DALLAS   MEXICO CITY   RIO DE JANEIRO

Time to Rejoice

Published in Nashville, Tennessee, by Thomas Nelson. Thomas Nelson is a trademark of Thomas Nelson, Inc.

Thomas Nelson, Inc., titles may be purchased in bulk for educational, business, fund-raising, or sales promotional use. For information, please e-mail SpecialMarkets@ ThomasNelson.com.

Scripture quotations are taken from THE ENGLISH STANDARD VERSION (ESV). © 2001 by Crossway Bibles, a division of Good News Publishers; HOLMAN CHRISTIAN STANDARD BIBLE (HCSB). © 1999, 2000, 2002, 2003 by Broadman and Holman Publishers. All rights reserved; KING JAMES VERSION (KJV); NEW AMERICAN STANDARD BIBLE® (NASB). © The Lockman Foundation 1960, 1962, 1963, 1968, 1971, 1972, 1973, 1975, 1977, 1995. Used by permission; NEW INTERNATIONAL VERSION® (NIV) © 1973, 1978, 1984 By International Bible Society. Used by permission of Zondervan Publishing House. All rights reserved; THE NEW KING JAMES VERSION (NKJV) © 1982 by Thomas Nelson, Inc. Used by permission. All rights reserved; NEW LIVING TRANSLATION (NLT) © 1996. Used by permission of Tyndale House Publishers, Inc., Wheaton, Illinois 60189. All rights reserved; The Message (MSG) by Eugene H. Peterson. © 1993, 1994, 1995, 1996, 2000. Used by permission of NavPress Publishing Group. All rights reserved; New Century Version® (NCV). © 2005 by Thomas Nelson, Inc. Used by permission. All rights reserved; THE CONTEMPORARY ENGLISH VERSION (CEV) © 1991 by the American Bible Society. Used by permission.

Some content by Sheila Walsh also appears in The Shelter of God's Promises © 2011 by Sheila Walsh.

"You Belong Here," by Chris Eaton and Kyle Matthews, © 2003 by Universal Music.

Library of Congress Cataloging-in-Publication Data

Time to rejoice : devotions celebrating God's love / Patsy Clairmont ... [et al.].
    p. cm.
 Includes bibliographical references and index.
 ISBN 978-1-4002-0294-2 (alk. paper)
 1. Christian women—Prayers and devotions. I. Clairmont, Patsy.
 BV4844.T56 2011
 242'.643—dc22   2010037502

Printed in the United States of America

11 12 13 14 15 QG 6 5 4 3 2 1

Contents

Comfort

Freedom

Assurance

Contents

INTRODUCTION

. . . .

Stories may be my favorite thing in life. I grew up in a storytelling family. We used to sit on the front porch every summer night, and neighbors and friends would gather. Daddy told story after story (some enhanced, I'm sure). Those are my best memories. Here I am, sixty-four years later, and real stories may be my favorite thing in life. God's great grace to me is that he has taught me so much about himself through stories: as recorded in the Scripture and from others who have learned how to walk with God by the way he has "shown up."

At Women of Faith, those who grace our platform tell wonderful stories—often about what went wrong in life and how they learned to put their trust in the all-loving, always-faithful God. Whenever we're together, at conferences on the weekends and throughout the many times our paths cross, we share what is happening in our lives and how God meets us and intersects our lives with his truth. If you are ever around me when I'm around the authors of this book you're holding, you will hear me say, "Tell them the one about . . ."

My hope is that you can take time to have a cup of tea or an iced cold drink and have a visit with some of the most important women I have ever known and the wonderful tales they have to relate. They will make you laugh or maybe make you cry a little, but always they will encourage you to rejoice in the fact of God's grace and love.

Mary Graham
Women of Faith President

The Greatness of God

1

The Soft Center of God's Greatness

. . . .

Lisa Harper

One of my all-time favorite pastors is a man named Roy Carter. I'm partial to Roy partly because he doesn't fit the *Saturday Night Live* stereotype of a man of the cloth. While he is a brilliant theologian—well versed in both ancient languages and modern-day application— he isn't stiff, joyless, or "religious." He doesn't have soft hands; he doesn't use corny, sentimental language; and he doesn't have a comb-over. Roy is garrulous and gregarious, a former semi-pro baseball player who-used-to-scout-for-the-Yankees kind of spiritual leader.

Not too long ago, he got distracted in the pulpit by the unmistakable sound of a cell phone ringing. At first Roy kept preaching and tried to ignore it, but within a minute or two, everyone in the congregation had become distracted too. People began shifting in their seats, eyeing suspiciously those sitting near the front of the sanctuary—where the ringing seemed to be coming from. One of the older members muttered audibly, "Good night, would somebody just turn the darn thing off!" Pretty soon the tension had become palpable. But then Roy grinned sheepishly and pulled the shrill culprit out of his own pocket.

In addition to that kind of charming authenticity, Roy tells really interesting stories that help me see God more clearly. He told one recently about a demanding professor, whom we'll call Dr. Impossible-to-Please for the sake of his tenure. Roy said Dr. Imp was the most exacting teacher he ever had. His subject matter—mastering the Hebrew language—was extremely difficult, and his standards were all but impossible. He assigned students a mountain of obscure texts to read and required every paper to be written according to literal publishing standards, complete with extensive annotated bibliographies.

Then, if they read the mounds of hieroglyphics until their eyes bled and they drank copious amounts of coffee to fuel multiple all-nighters in order to write an intelligent and comprehensive response that perfectly adhered to publishing protocol but just so happened to be a fraction of an inch off on the margins of said paper, Dr. Imp knocked a full letter grade off before reading it. Suffice it to say, he refused to even accept papers that students tried to turn in late.

Which is why Roy and the rest of his classmates winced

when a fellow seminarian humbly asked Dr. Imp for an extension on his final thesis, which was due the following day, explaining that his wife was hospitalized with complications stemming from her first pregnancy. Of course, as they all dreaded, Dr. Imp said, "I'm sorry, son, but you'll still have to turn in your paper tomorrow." He refused to budge on his no-tardy-assignments rule.

The next day, after most of the class had gathered in little indignant clumps in the hallway and skewered the professor with impassioned accusations, they found out the rest of the story. How Dr. Imp had approached the beleaguered young husband immediately after class and asked for his address. And how a few hours later he drove across town to the soon-to-be-parents' apartment and typed the paper himself. Dr. Seemingly-Impossible-to-Please set a very high bar for his students, yet he had the mercy to hold it in place with his own hands.

You can imagine where Roy went next. He explained that while the Old Testament demands the impossibly exorbitant ticket price of moral perfection in order for us to gain access to God, God chose to pay the price out of his own pocket . . . out of his own heart. Before God stretched out the canvas of sky, hung the stars in place, and set our galaxy in motion, he also arranged to satisfy our entrance fee with his only begotten Son. God never relaxed his standard of holiness, but he's the one who fulfilled it on our behalf.

I can't remember the scripture Roy turned to after sharing that real-life illustration, but I can tell you the one it reminds me of. It reminds me of this true tale at the beginning of the divine love story we've been written into:

> After this, the word of the LORD came to Abram in a vision:
>
> "Do not be afraid, Abram.
>
> I am your shield,
>
> your very great reward."
>
> But Abram said, "O Sovereign LORD, what can you give me since I remain childless and the one who will inherit my estate is Eliezer of Damascus?" And Abram said, "You have given me no children; so a servant in my household will be my heir."
>
> Then the word of the LORD came to him: "This man will not be your heir, but a son coming from your own body will be your heir." He took him outside and said, "Look up at the heavens and count the stars—if indeed you can count them." Then he said to him, "So shall your offspring be." Abram believed the LORD, and he credited it to him as righteousness. (Genesis 15:1–6 NIV)

Now you probably remember this part of Abraham and Sarah's bio; they're both so old at this point that they're wearing Depends, but then God basically says, "Cheer up and go buy some Pampers because you two are going to have a baby!" And initially Abe believed God's audacious announcement. But then he mulled over Jehovah's projected miracle a little bit more—all the while noticing through the bottom half of his bifocals how dark the liver spots were on Sarah's hands—and his faith began to waver. "But Abram said, 'O Sovereign LORD, how can I know that I will gain possession of it?'" (Genesis 15:8 NIV).

Yet instead of whacking Abraham on the knuckles as punishment for his trust tremors, God tips his hand and lovingly gives the old guy a peek at the Living Hope that's right around the corner:

> So the LORD said to him, "Bring me a heifer, a goat and a ram, each three years old, along with a dove and a young pigeon."
>
> Abram brought all these to him, cut them in two and arranged the halves opposite each other; the birds, however, he did not cut in half. Then birds of prey came down on the carcasses, but Abram drove them away.
>
> As the sun was setting, Abram fell into a deep sleep, and a thick and dreadful darkness came over him. . . .
>
> When the sun had set and darkness had fallen, a smoking firepot with a blazing torch appeared and passed between the pieces. On that day the LORD made a covenant with Abram and said, "To your descendants I give this land, from the river of Egypt to the great river,

the Euphrates—the land of the Kenites, Kenizzites, Kadmonites, Hittites, Perizzites, Rephaites, Amorites, Canaanites, Girgashites and Jebusites." (Genesis 15:9–12, 17–21 NIV)

This dissection ceremony that seems so foreign and repugnant now was actually very familiar to Abraham (you'll notice he doesn't declare, "Say what?" when God gives him directions). He had probably participated in this messy custom many times before because this was one of the ways ancient cultures enacted a binding contract between two parties. By cutting the animals in half and then walking through the blood runoff in bare feet, the two sides were solemnly illustrating what should happen to them if they broke their agreement. Sort of the biblical version of the way when we were young that we'd poke our thumb with a safety pin and press it together with a friend's to become "blood buddies."

The truly unique part of this pact was that Abraham snored through the entire event. His feet never touched the crimson trail. A smoking firepot and a flaming torch—which are *theophanies* or physical manifestations of God—are the only things that passed between the parts. By walking through without Abraham, God tangibly demonstrated that he and he alone would keep the covenant between himself and mankind. He knew we'd break our vows, get distracted by shiny things, and struggle with submitting to his authority. God knew perfect worship and obeisance were way beyond our ability. So he didn't make Abraham trudge through. Our Creator knew even then that Jesus' blood was the price he'd eventually have to pay to reconcile us into a right relationship with himself.

Just imagine the sigh of relief Roy and his classmates would've breathed if, immediately after explaining the most stringent rules in the syllabus, Dr. Imp had said with a wink, "But don't worry y'all—if you mess up, I've got your back!"

God's mercy is at the very core of his greatness.

"Give thanks to the Lord and proclaim his greatness. Let the whole world know what he has done" (Psalm 105:1 NLT).

2

Looking Back

. . . .

Luci Swindoll

For most of my life, I've been nearsighted. I've read the tiniest print without blinking an eye and painted minuscule letters on art projects with no problem. As time went on, I became farsighted. I could spot moving vehicles w-aaa-y down the road and read street signs from a distance. However, now that I'm in my seventies and my eyes are negatively affected by aging, my best vision is hindsighted. I feel a bit like the apostle Paul when he wrote to the early church, in Romans 15:17: "Looking back over what has been accomplished and what I have observed, I must say I am most pleased—in the context of Jesus, I'd even say *proud*, but only in that context" (MSG).

Of course, hindsight is the easiest sight of all. We've got the full picture of what went on because we're *looking back on what's been accomplished and observed* as Paul says. And as I look back on my life, over and over I can see the greatness of God on my behalf, as he has brought me through ups and downs, to the place I am today. Nothing has been a mistake and there are no regrets. Now.

In many ways, my life has been what I envisioned and planned when I was younger, yet different. I can recall times when I was aware God was working in this or that, but I didn't know I'd need to go through what I did in order to get where I am today. As E. M. Forster wrote, "We must be willing to let go of the life we have planned, so as to have the life that is waiting for us." I believe that statement in every sense of the word.

Thirty-seven years ago, when I moved from Texas to California, I was going to take the world by storm. Up to that point, I had spent all my life in Texas, and now I would be living in an entirely new and different environment. I had been working in a research laboratory (which I totally enjoyed) and now I would be involved in another branch of Mobil Oil—and had fully intended to enjoy it as well. Boy! Was I fooled! Within two weeks after getting settled in a new apartment and launching into a new job, I was miserable. *Nothing* was like it had been before. Where there was lots of stimulating discussion in the research lab, there was now a virtual "code of silence" in my new office. Where I had dashed half a mile down the road to go to work in Dallas, I now had to get on the Los Angeles freeway system before dawn to drive for an hour . . . and make the return trip home. Where I had numerous friends with whom I spent time after work and on weekends, I now knew only a few people on the West Coast. *But God knew all of this.*

The battle between my dreams and reality went on for four years, and I can't tell you the number of times I was ready to throw in the towel. I cried, compared, and complained—all the while wondering what had possessed me to make this change in location. I was heartsick when I got up in the morning and when I went to bed at night. I simply couldn't believe my judgment had been so wrong.

One morning on my way to work, I told the Lord *once again* how dissatisfied I was. I asked him to change my life—any kind of change would do. *"I want to do something significant,"* I said. *"I want to make a difference; not sit behind a drafting table forever. And Lord, I'd so appreciate your telling me 'This is it,' when it comes along because I don't want to miss it. Honestly, I'm leaving this with you now, Lord, and I mean it this time."*

I'm not kidding, that very night my brother Chuck invited me to have dinner at his home to meet someone from Multnomah Press, for whom Chuck was writing books. It was during that evening that this gentleman asked me to write my first book, and God very clearly said in my heart: *"This is it, Luci. Just say yes!"* It was as if God had been waiting for me to pray that prayer so he could get to work on this request. After a bit of conversation and being convinced that this was the Lord prompting me, I said yes. That *yes* opened a whole new world for me. A world I never ever expected, and a new (and very personal) way of looking at how great God is and how he is interested in our welfare and circumstances—the pain in our hearts, the disappointment in our lives, the fear of never getting out of the mess we've made, the longing for something better.

All sorts of doors began to open. When I finished writing that book, I had invitations to write others. And to speak. And to travel. The irony of this whole story is that shortly after my first book came out and while I was still working as a draftsman for Mobil, I was called into the chief executive's office one afternoon and told I was being considered for another job. It was entirely different from the drafting job I had been doing for the past four years. Needless to say, I was very surprised. I'd not been told that particular job was being offered, nor that I was being considered for it. However, there I was, being asked by the big boss if I was interested in becoming a rights of way and claims agent. *Mercy! What IS a rights of way and claims agent*, I wondered.

"Do you like to meet people?" That was his first question.

"Would you be willing to go back to school to take courses in appraisal, engineering, negotiation, and real estate law?"

And finally, "Will you work overtime when the need arises?"

My answer to all those questions was a resounding Yes! So, I was given the job, worked in it for seven years, and loved it. But here's the ironic part—there wasn't a single day I could have done that work had I not learned what I did in the job I hated. Who knew? God did. Remember . . . God knew that, and he never let me out of his sight.

When my rights of way supervisor retired, I was asked to be the manager of that department—the first woman in an executive position on Mobil's West Coast team. God has his own way of doing things, and more often than not, that way doesn't fall into our preconceived category. In fact, I took early retirement from Mobil in order to do what I've now been doing for the past twenty-five years. And sixteen years ago I started speaking with Women of Faith . . . the apex of my speaking ministry and one of the best gifts God has ever given me.

That said, my friends, I want to make this point really clear: you have no idea how God in his greatness and love is going to use what he is taking you through now to mature you and bring you out on the other side. Sometimes we haven't a clue "where this is gonna lead," but I can tell you from experience, if God is in it, there are reasons far greater than the dream you have for your own life.

Every period of life has a purpose: Sometimes it's just to endure. Other times it's to thrive. And others are given for us to grow. But you can be sure our great God knows the difference, is with us in all of them, and is not making a mistake about anything.

And may I also say—don't allow regret to get a stronghold

in your life. Some people feel regret gives insight. I disagree. Regret causes us to bog down. We become immovable when we live with regret. We sit around, longing for what never was, and it kills the energy to get up, keep at it, and move on to the next thing. God cannot make a mistake with our lives. He has the foresight that we lack, and he uses it as he plans our lives. William Cowper's poem "Light Shining Out of Darkness" says it beautifully:

> *God moves in a mysterious way*
> *His wonders to perform;*
> *He plants his footsteps in the sea,*
> *And rides upon the storm.*
>
> *Deep in unfathomable mines*
> *Of never-failing skill,*
> *He treasures up his bright designs,*
> *And works his sovereign will.*
>
> *His purposes will ripen fast,*
> *Unfolding every hour;*
> *The bud may have a bitter taste,*
> *But sweet will be the flower.*
>
> *Blind unbelief is sure to err,*
> *And scan his work in vain:*
> *God is his own interpreter,*
> *And he will make it plain!*

3

Watching for God

. . . .

Mandisa

Since becoming a professional recording artist, I have had some pretty memorable moments onstage. I'll never forget gazing out at the unforgettable view of the ocean on a cruise ship as I sang "Awesome God." The memory of seeing congregations from various denominations, races, and communities dancing with me as I sang "Love Somebody" in Monroe, Louisiana, will forever be etched in my mind. And belting out my song about heaven, "Only the World," on the *Regis and Kelly* show just months after my elimination from *American Idol* is something I will always be grateful for.

Easter 2010 will also be something I will never forget. Generally, when someone wants to book me for an event, my agent collects all of the information, then sends it to me so I can pray over the request. I remember when my manager first told me about this petition. New Hope

Church on the Hawaiian island Oahu requested me and my band for Easter weekend. My prayer went something like this: "Dear Lord, I really wanna go. Okay? Amen"!

I'll never forget the sounds, smells, and sights that greeted me when I stepped off of the plane in Honolulu. Even though we had spent an exhausting ten hours on an airplane, my fellow travelers and I were buzzing with excited chatter. I could smell the lovely scent of flowers wafting on the breeze. It was an ideal seventy-seven degrees, and the sky was the perfect combination of blue with puffy white clouds. I knew the next seven days would be some of the best of my life. And they were! I swam with dolphins, ate the freshest seafood and produce I've ever had, and met some of the most joy-filled people in existence (locals would simply describe this as the "aloha spirit").

Ah, and the sights! I'm convinced there are colors that only exist in Hawaii. The vivid pinks, purples, and yellows I saw in the leis wrapped around tourists' necks evoked a feeling of giddiness in me. The green foliage of Lanikai Point rustled in the massive wind that was sweeping across the state. And the crystal blue water was so clear I could see straight through to the bottom of the ocean.

On the second day of our vacation, my friends and I spent the day at Waikiki beach. After soaking up the hot sun, we decided to swim out as far as we could. We quickly discovered that we were swimming right over a coral reef. It was simply awe inspiring as I spied fish of shocking colors and shapes. As I grew more comfortable with the sight, I drank in the brilliant picture I was experiencing. Some of the fish were so outrageous they caused me to come up for air to get a good laugh in. One such critter that evoked this reaction was a turquoise fish with tiny pink spots and a nose about an inch long. (Wait a minute. Do fish have noses? They don't! They have gills. What was that thing?) It was so ugly, it was beautiful! Who could come up with such a creature? I marveled at the cleverness of God. He truly is a brilliant artist, and I was blessed to enjoy his masterpiece. I saw dozens of different types of fish in that little cross-section of coral reef. I could only imagine the variety that exists throughout the entire expanse of the ocean. God is not only creative—he must have a sense of humor too!

Since my time in Hawaii, I have often thought about how God does things so differently than I would. I have read Isaiah 55:8–9 for years: "'For my thoughts are not your thoughts, neither are your ways my ways,' declares the LORD. 'As the heavens are higher than the earth, so are my ways higher than your ways and my thoughts than your thoughts'" (NIV). But somehow, seeing the manifestation of God's thoughts swimming before me in the ocean has made that scripture come to life. I can savor his imagination in the beauty of his creation. And when I face circumstances that look hopeless, I am learning to appreciate his wisdom and to trust his plan.

One such situation where I am challenged to trust in God's sovereignty is with the salvation of my brother. When I think about Jesus' return to earth, I am split between begging for him to hurry and pleading for him to tarry for the sake of my brother. I pray for my brother regularly, and at times I try to think of creative ways for God to get his attention. Maybe my brother can fall in love with a Christian woman who won't enter into a relationship with him because they are unequally yoked. Or what if God would speak to him in a dream. Or how about after a hot shower, he sees a finger writing John 3:16 on the steamy mirror. In the end, I usually conclude my prayers with a confession of trust, recognizing that God may not make himself known the way I want him to, but I have faith that he will indeed make himself known.

When God does show up, I want to recognize him. I love the story of how God showed up in Elijah's life in 1 Kings 19.

> The LORD said, "Go out and stand on the mountain in the presence of the LORD, for the LORD is about to pass by." Then a great and powerful wind tore the mountains apart and shattered the rocks before the LORD, but the LORD was not in the wind. After the wind there was an earthquake, but the LORD was not in the earthquake. After the earthquake came a fire, but the LORD

was not in the fire. And after the fire came a gentle whisper. (vv. 11–12 NIV)

God didn't appear in a forceful wind, a mighty earthquake, or a blazing fire. He showed up in a way that one would least expect. (Similarly, I don't believe many expected the Messiah to come in the form of a baby born in a stable either! God is just full of surprises, isn't he?) I imagine that Elijah had to crane his neck to hear God's still, small voice. Maybe that is why the Lord chose to come that way. After all, you'd be hard-pressed to miss an earthquake or a fire, but hearing a whisper requires one to draw close. It involves intimacy.

I don't know how God will capture the attention of my brother and bring him into a relationship, and I'll continue to pray for God's intervention. I will most likely continue to make suggestions to God every now and then, but I am excited to see my extravagant God in action. I rest knowing that the Father desires a relationship with my brother just as God longs for that closeness with each of us. As I anticipate the day of my brother's salvation, I'll continue to marvel at the extraordinary, creative, and sometimes humorous way God wields his power to those of us who are watching.

4

Moving from Sad to Glad

. . . .

Patsy Clairmont

Outside my window is a bush of Rose of Sharon whose blooms are usually quite sanguine, but not today. A summer shower came through, and now the blooms hang like teardrops. I know that, later, the blossoms will smile again, but for now they weep purple puddles.

And isn't that how it is with us?

Things are looking good when an unexpected shower rains on our parade, and sometimes it's hard to rebound and lift our heads back toward the sun. So, we sink into our sad.

That's what happened to Elijah. He had a mountain-top experience—and I'm talking literally here, girls; you've read about it in 1 Kings 18. It was like one of those old Westerns so dear to my heart. On this side of the mountain, in the black hats: the priests of Baal. Four hundred and fifty of them! On the other side, looming out of the dust like a biblical Clint Eastwood, the lone good guy: Elijah. All around them: the citizens of Israel.

This particular shootout didn't involve firearms or arrows. Their weapon of choice was bull. I mean, bulls. The four-legged kind. The baddies (or would they be Baalies?) went first. They built an altar, cut up their cow (er, bull), and asked their god to turn on the stove. When that didn't work, they asked louder. Nothing. They jumped around, in case that might catch his attention. No dice. Then they asked some more. *Nada.* Verse 26 says they "called on the name of Baal from morning even till noon" (NKJV). (Don't you know their throats hurt?)

When it got to be lunchtime and the meat was still raw and probably disgusting (I imagine it was covered in flies and starting to smell by this point), Elijah began to offer a few helpful suggestions. Don't you love it when people offer you "helpful" advice when you're trying to do something? Especially when it's not going well? Me neither.

Elijah's advice was pretty snarky too. Maybe he was hungry, or he'd gotten up too early for his big showdown. Maybe he just wanted to get on to his part of the program. His suggestions went along the lines of "Yell louder, boys! Maybe he's asleep, or thinking about something else, or on vacation." Yeah, that's helpful.

The Baalies kept doing what they were doing until evening. Can I tell you that when what you're doing isn't working over the long term, it might be time to try something else? Somebody defined insanity as "doing the same thing over and over again and expecting a different result." By the time dusk fell, the priests of Baal were probably pretty much out of their minds, what with all the shouting and jumping and cutting themselves around their heap of raw bull.

Then came Elijah's big moment, the one he'd been waiting for all day. He told all the people, "Come over here." When he had a good audience gathered, he built his own altar, cut up his own bull, and drenched the whole thing with water. He didn't just sprinkle a little bit, either; we're talking buckets of water. He had to dig a moat around the altar just to collect the runoff. When everything was as wet as it could be and the moat was brimful, Elijah asked God to show up and let everyone know who was God. And God showed up big-time! Whoosh! Fire came down from heaven and promptly burned up Elijah's offering. It even dried up all the water in the moat. It was crystal clear to everyone there that the Lord was God.

Now, wouldn't you think the next chapter would have Elijah waving at cheering crowds from atop a camel sporting the Grand Marshal banner in the Israel Homecoming Parade? Instead, Queen Jezebel told her posse to find Elijah and hang him high, which caused our hero to run scared. Literally. He ran for miles and miles into the desert until he found a tree to flop under. Then he announced to his sandy surroundings, "Take me now, Lord, I'm ready to die" and went to sleep. (He'd had a big day, after all.)

Have you ever felt like that? I have. For years I dragged my sorry self around like a bag of old potatoes, weighed down by an inexplicable sadness. Like Elijah, I had days when I took to my bed, kind of hoping I wouldn't wake up. I was so down, I couldn't even see up from there. Then I slowly began to realize I was a big influence on myself, and I could make some changes that would help lift my own spirit.

Here's a partial list. Some of these things sound too simple to matter, but give them a try and see if they don't promote goodwill in your own heart and home.

Sing: No, it doesn't matter if your voice sounds like fingernails on chalkboards, just sing. And don't go singing the blues. Choose happy songs that, once upon a time, made your toe tap and your heart skip. Put on a Women of Faith praise CD and worship the Lord. Earn extra points (and burn extra calories) if you dance around the room while you tra-la-la.

Warning: if you are in the doldrums, you won't feel like doing this at first, but with all the love in the world, may I suggest you do it anyway. (Don't make me come over there.)

Laugh: Call up a funny friend, watch a funny movie, read a funny book—whatever tickles your fancy and stirs up some health-producing endorphins. Deliberately lighten up. It's a choice, and one you *can* make. Pretend if you have to! Many a time, I started out phonily happy and ended up genuinely joyful.

Serve: Do something for someone else; it gets our minds off us. Bake a cake, send a card, plan a party for someone you love or don't, pick a bouquet for a neighbor (out of your own yard, please, not theirs!), take a group to a Women of Faith event. Brightening someone else's day results in reflected brightness shining on your own.

Study: Pick a Bible passage to study, then memorize one of the verses that cheers you. God's Word changes our minds and strengthens our fragile characters. The verses hidden in your heart tend to pop out into your mind when you need them most.

Create: There's something about working with one's mind and heart in a creative manner that releases bad vibes and restores the soul. You don't have to be an artist to create—I promise. I did watercolors for a couple of years before I painted something identifiable. It startled me when I recognized my effort. I showed a friend, and we immediately framed and hung it.

Maybe you'd rather cook, bake, garden, dance, sew, scrapbook—okay, do it. It's not about making something art-gallery worthy; it's about enjoying yourself. You don't have to show anyone your efforts unless you just want to.

Avoid: Pity parties. Newscasts. Negative people. When Jesus went to heal a dying daughter, he kicked out all the mourners and only took three disciples and the girl's parents with him. If Jesus avoided negative Nellies, we should too. Other things that can send you on a downward spiral are: Racy books. Overeating. Sad movies. Excuses. (Ouch! I'm so good at that last one too.)

While it's not easy to move out of sad, I hope these few reminders help to improve the quality of your inner atmosphere. Oh wait—there's more: pray, exercise, clean house, journal, volunteer, rest . . . (somebody stop me!).

By the way, in case you're wondering about Elijah sleeping out there in the desert, the next morning he got a wake-up call from an angel, who brought him breakfast in bed, no less. You'd think that would have cheered him up, wouldn't you? It would me. For some reason God never sends me a message reading, "Get up and eat." Usually it's more along the lines of, "Put that down. Step away from the muffin."

Elijah, on the other hand, was so down in the dumps that it took another divine donut delivery and a couple of pity parties before he managed to crawl out of his sad and do something productive. (Eventually God told him, "Your chariot awaits," and off he went in a blaze of glory, but that's another story.)

Don't stay miserable; it's no fun there. So dab away those tears, roll up the sleeves of your determination, and start moving from sad to glad. It's worth the effort. And that's no bull.

5

Our Giving God

. . . .

Marilyn Meberg

I have a new bust. When I made that announcement to some friends recently, each said, "About time." If you and I have a long track record, you will remember I squished my silicone implants ten years ago. I was merely crossing an intersection when I stumbled and with enormous velocity hit the pavement in a full body press. It completely knocked the air out of my lungs, sent my top teeth slicing through my lower lip, and rearranged my bust configuration.

This was life-changing on many fronts. To begin with, the damaged implants had to be surgically removed. Shortly after their removal, I experienced a six-month-long reaction to the toxicity of silicone, which sidelined me to my bed and then to a chair. Shakily I moved on with my life and returned to my original flat-chested self.

That said, let's move on to a description of my new bust. It is heavy and made of Italian white marble.

What does my new bust look like? The sculpture is the head of a young girl whose gaze is slightly averted to the left. The expression on her face brings tears to my eyes. She looks pensive, as if she has been sobered by sad news. But there is still serenity in her expression that indicates she will not be defeated by whatever the nature of her life experience.

Her face is flawlessly chiseled, and I am utterly charmed by it. She inspires equal amounts of encouragement, empathy, curiosity, and even peace in me. In addition to the nearly beatific expression on her face, I am astounded by the head scarf in which she is shrouded. It has ruffles. How in the world can marble be chiseled to look as if it has ruffles? The ruffles appear to be the result of a slight breeze. From a distance, one would think the scarf is made of taffeta instead of marble. It is perfection in every detail.

I know almost nothing about this marvelous piece of sculpture except that it is Italian marble from the eighteenth century. I came across it as a result of a friend of mine who with her husband made numerous trips to Europe every year and brought home "rare finds" to be sold in their shop. With the death of her husband, the owner decided the business was too much for her, so an Everything Must Go sign was placed in the window.

But here's the reason I am telling you about "Eve."

(I named her Eve because she appears to have her original innocence but with her disobedience of God she's beginning to realize the enormity of her decision and its far-reaching consequences. I know, I know. Sometimes I'm a bit much.) I have had a spiritual battle over the fact that I purchased this sculpture. I did not "need" her certainly because the pedestal on which she sits looked fine without her. This purchase of mine was simply motivated by a strong "I desperately want to have that piece; it speaks to my soul and moves my spirit!" But now that I have it, I keep thinking about how many World Vision children I could have sponsored with the money I selfishly spent on bringing Eve into my home.

Do you ever struggle over what you "have" and think maybe you should not have whatever the "it" is? If you do, we are floating around in the same boat. However, I am beginning to grasp a truth I think I used to know but forgot. At least the side trip to this truth feels familiar. (My life would be less troubled if I didn't keep forgetting what I think I learned one time.)

I have a rich biblical heritage. My dad was a pastor; my mom taught women's Bible studies all her adult life; the Bible was central to every phase of my growing-up years. I went to a Christian university, married a Christian man, and gave birth to kids who became Christians. Now, at the age of seventy-one, I continue to place my faith in the God of my youth and the teachings of the Bible. I am a sincere Christian woman. So why, then, do I falter with the straightforward statement of Romans 8:32: "Since he did not spare even his own Son but gave him up for us all, won't he also give us everything else?" (NLT). What about: "Teach those who are rich in this world not to be proud and not to trust in their money, which is so unreliable. Their trust should be in God, who richly gives us all we need for our enjoyment" (1 Timothy 6:17 NLT).

I tend to slide over phrases like "why would he not give us everything else" and "God gives us all we need for our enjoyment." I think I slide over them because I don't want to be materialistic or risk living outside the central purpose of my life that is to honor God.

The challenge here is for me to be balanced in my faith, recognizing that, of course, I am not to place higher value on "stuff" than I do on God. His first commandment was "You must not have any other God but me." But here is the balancing and liberating truth of Scripture that I sometimes forget: God is a huge giver! He gave us Jesus, who rescues us from the sin that separates us from God. With the gift of Jesus, God is also the giver of other good things. In fact, he is the primary giver of all good things: scenic beauty, sunshine, fresh air, great food, laughter, reading, music, relationships, the ocean . . . I could go on and on. Every good thing has its origin in God. Those good things are experienced in an earthly environment.

The ability to experience joy is yet another of God's

gifts to me. It, too, has its origin in God. If I were not designed to experience joy, those capacities would be sealed off like a soul bottle cap. Joy could not surface. Why? It would not exist. If God had not created the capacity to experience joy, life would be reduced to a monotone existence: no color, vibrancy, curiosity, excitement, variety. I would slog through my days not even knowing a good cup of tea with a friend could produce joy; add a square of chocolate and the joy could shoot through the roof. But I'd know nothing about that simple pleasure if God had not gifted me with the capacity to experience joy. Because there is no soul bottle cap, the sky's the limit.

So now I'm going to walk myself through how I can keep my God-given joy capacity balanced. Should I be feeling guilty about my new bust?

I should feel guilt if it causes me to go into threatening or destructive debt. I should feel guilt if it (and other stuff) means more to me than my relationship with God. I should feel guilt if I don't tithe income and even extend over the top to share with others. I should feel guilt if I don't know when to stop buying busts and my house fills up with soulful-looking marble women.

Not feeling guilt, on the other hand, rests entirely on the fact that God gives me all things to enjoy. To refuse his gift is to forget that those gifts inspire gratitude and thanksgiving. When I feel gratitude and thanksgiving, I express that in my prayers and in my spirit. That gift provides a sweet communion between my Father and me. All of God's gifts are given to me in love. It pleases the heart of God to give joyful experiences to his children. On the other hand, what would not please the heart of God is if I did not acknowledge the source of all good and joy-producing gifts and appreciate them.

I am reminded there is a godless legalism that can easily creep into our hearts and minds when we get out of balance in receiving God's gifts. That legalism causes us to distrust pleasure. The movie *Babette's Feast* brilliantly illustrates godless legalism. The story line centers on two sisters in nineteenth-century Denmark who live with their pastor father. The tiny church he serves is fearful of anything that produces pleasure; to them pleasure leads to sin. The sisters agree never to leave their father, and after his death they continue teaching the joyless system he believed.

After some years a French woman, Babette, arrives at their door, begs them to take her in, and commits herself to work for them as maid and cook. The sisters are uncertain: she is Catholic and French, but they relent. They painstakingly discourage her French cooking flair and try to teach her the plain and unseasoned recipes approved by God.

When the sisters decide to hold a dinner to commemorate the hundredth anniversary of their father's birth, Babette begs the sisters to allow her to take charge of the preparation of the meal. They are concerned about what Babette might serve, but they allow her to go ahead. Babette then prepares the feast of a lifetime for the members of the tiny church.

Though initially hesitant, the church people ultimately relax and are then overwhelmed and delighted with the never-before-experienced flavors and textures of the meal served to them. They begin to enjoy their food and each other as well. Soon everyone is experiencing an earthly pleasure beyond any they'd ever known. Amazingly enough, it does not lead to sin.

When Jesus was on this earth, he challenged his listeners to enlarge their understanding on the topic of God's gifts when he said: "If you then, being evil, know how to give good gifts to your children, how much more will your Father who is in heaven give good things to those who ask Him!" (Matthew 7:11 NKJV).

I've enjoyed writing this devotional; it has prodded me to get back on track as I'm reminded of God's pleasure in limitless giving. Just a minute ago, I walked over to the pedestal upon which Eve sits. As I stroked the bust without a trace of silicone, I said, "Thank you, Jesus. This soul-satisfying sculpture is a gift from you. I am grateful." I concluded my little praise service with my favorite tea sipped from my grandmother's porcelain teacup—pure pleasure.

6

Bring What You Have

. . . .

Sheila Walsh

"How many loaves do you have?" he asked. "Go and see."
—Mark 6:38 NIV

Christian was about to turn four, and his father, Barry, and I were in full planning mode. William, my father-in-law, had been living with us since his wife died the previous year, so he was highly invested in this birthday bash as well. We were sitting at the breakfast table, each with our own copy of the local *Parenting* magazine open to the classified section.

"What about a clown?" William suggested.

"That might be good," I said. "Although sometimes clowns can be a little creepy."

"I think he'd like a jumpy-inflatable-castle thing," Barry said.

"Yes, those are always fun," I agreed. "I've heard great things, too, about this guy who comes from the zoo with a selection of small animals and teaches the kids about them."

"How small?" Barry asked.

"Well . . . like raccoons and lizards and small snakes," I said.

"Snakes!" William said with a shiver. "Man, I hate snakes."

"What about this?" Barry said, holding the page open to a picture of two llamas.

"What do they do?" William asked.

"They give pony rides except they are llamas, so llama rides, I guess," Barry replied.

"I like that," I said.

Finally we narrowed it down to six possibilities. Barry said he would make inquiries and see what was available for the date we wanted and what the cost would be. I sent out the invitations and ordered the cake and prayed for a sunny day. As the birthday got closer, I asked Barry which entertainment option he had settled on, but he said that he wanted it to be a surprise. The phrase "Oh foolish Galatians" came to mind, but I ignored it.

The day arrived, and it was picture-perfect. The party was scheduled from 2:00 to 5:00 p.m., and at 1:30 p.m. a van pulled into our driveway. I saw that it had "Party Inflatables" on the side.

"Great choice, Barry," I said. "Christian will love this!"

Barry looked a little confused, but I put that down to the thought of the impending stampede of four-year-olds about to flatten our lawn. Christian ran around the yard, beside himself with excitement as he saw the giant inflatable castle take shape. William stationed himself at the front door to welcome our guests as they began to arrive, and I showed the children and their moms out into the backyard.

"Sheila!"

I heard William call my name with an edge of concern, and I hurried to the front door. William pointed down the driveway where two girls stood holding the reins of three ponies. Another girl stood on the doorstep.

"Hi!" I said. "Are these for the Walsh party?"

She assured me that they were, and I led them around the side of the house to the backyard. Christian and his friends were so excited, and they lined up to take turns at riding the docile animals.

Okay, so he booked the castle and the ponies, I thought. *That's fun; you don't turn four every day.*

"Sheila!"

I arrived back at the front door in time to see a woman wearing a fire-engine-red wig and a big red nose. A loud horn announced her arrival with three short but profound blasts.

"Are you here for the Walsh party?" I asked incredulously.

One deafening honk was her reply.

I decided that this might be an opportune moment to ask Barry why half of the city's children's party crowd had stationed themselves at our house, but I didn't have time.

"Sheila!"

I was almost afraid to go. William stood at the door, looking as if a truck had hit him as "Jungle Jim" began to unload his menagerie of small zoo animals. Before I had a chance to ask him the obligatory question, "Penelope the Face Painter" arrived.

I'd love to tell you that it ended there, but there was one more surprise. The children had all taken turns on the ponies and were painted every color under the sun. They had bounced up a storm and laughed at the clown's exceedingly bad jokes and were now sitting on the floor in the den in a half circle to listen to "Jungle Jim." William was by this time shaking his head. I heard the front door bell and thought, *I may never answer the door again.* I opened the door to be greeted by a very harried-looking man who immediately apologized for being late. Behind him stood two huge llamas!

As the children filed out that day, they all declared it the best party they had ever been to. The mothers did not look so thrilled. "What are we supposed to do now for our parties?" one asked. "Book the space shuttle?" I muttered something about leaving it all up to Barry and the book of Galatians and that I was sure we would never have a party again. When every last critter had been gathered up, including the six-foot-long albino python, and every horn had been silenced, I found Barry sitting in the den with his head in his hands.

"What on earth was that?" I asked. "We just had sixteen critters in our home, and I'm not even counting the clown! Every mother in the neighborhood now sees me as the enemy. What happened?"

"I didn't mean to," he said in a whisper.

"What do you mean?" I asked. "Did they all just volunteer their gifts?"

"Well . . . I asked them all to hold the date until I decided which one I wanted, and I forgot to get back to the others when I made my decision," he said.

"So which one had you decided on?" I asked.

"The llamas," he replied. "Just the llamas."

We looked at each other and fell on the floor laughing.

Compare this party to the one that took place on the hillside with Christ, his disciples, and five thousand men. It must have been a little like the children at the party—*more* just kept coming. For the children, it wasn't just an inflatable castle, but ponies, and a clown, and . . . The crowd with Jesus ate until they were filled—and *more* just kept coming.

The disciples got a lesson on that day about the greatness of God. As the sun began to set, the disciples were tired, and they urged Jesus to wrap up his teaching and send the people away. They were hungry, and they were tired and they had had enough. "Now when it was evening, the disciples came to him and said, 'This is a desolate place, and the day is now over; send the crowds away to go into the villages and buy food for themselves'" (Matthew 14:15 ESV).

The Synoptic Gospels (Matthew, Mark, and Luke) all record that Jesus turned to the disciples and told them, "You give them something to eat." Can you imagine the size of the crowd? If there were five thousand men and you add in wives and children, widows, and single women, we are looking at a crowd of at least ten thousand people. How on earth could they do that?

The fact is, they couldn't. As the disciples looked at Jesus in disbelief at what he was asking them to do, Jesus asked: "How many loaves do you have? Go and see" (Mark 6:38 NIV).

Like the disciples, so often we are overwhelmed by what we don't have instead of what Christ has given us. All God asks us to do is bring what we have and let him do what only he can do.

I am often flooded with a sense of what I don't have. But I have learned, like the little boy on a hillside who brought only a basket of fish and loaves of bread one day, that all Jesus asks us to bring is what we do have and to leave the rest up to our great God. When we do that, like a birthday party that began with an inflatable castle and ended with so much more, our lives turn into a fabulous celebration.

7

Family Reunion

....

Lisa Whelchel

*O*ne of my favorite, yet seldom-used, words to describe Jesus is "inclusive." He didn't gather up a little group of people who were all Jewish, worshipped him as the Son of God, attended synagogue weekly, and believed all the same "rules" of morality. Quite the opposite. He not only accepted and embraced people where they were, but he went even further and invited them into his circle and offered them access to his heart. To Jesus, being in the family of God is easy: "Follow me," he said.

Nothing else matters.

In the family of God, Jesus doesn't require us to be rich. Or good-looking. Or popular. Or talented. And in this family, we are welcomed in all our diversity. Some *are* rich. Some *are* good-looking. Some *are* popular. Some *are* talented. And some aren't. But we are *all* welcomed—we are *all* loved.

I really saw how that works one weekend when we had a family reunion at my mother's cabin in east Texas— and I use the word *cabin* loosely. Think, room with a sofa bed connected to a room with a sink connected to a room with a potty. Then imagine forty aunts, uncles, cousins, sisters, brothers, sons, daughters, and various in-laws all collecting inside to get out of a sudden thunderstorm.

It was a wonderful weekend. The first night was just the immediate family: my mom, stepdad, brother, sister-in-law, halfbrother, new sister-in-law, nephew, husband, son and his girlfriend, and daughters and their boyfriends. Definitely a crowd but an intimate gathering compared to what was ahead.

We reserved a long table at Catfish Cove. The table was already set with two types of hush puppies, slaw, and french fries. There were also three squirt bottles: one filled with ketchup, one with tartar sauce, and one with liquid butter (presumably to put on the fried hush puppies). All that was before we even ordered the all-you-can-eat fried catfish plate. Yes, this was a heart-attack-waiting-to-happen kind of place.

The next morning, the rest of the kinfolks started arriving. There were new babies to cuddle, new husbands to introduce, and new teenagers to not recognize. We spent the first morning hanging out around the dock. Some of the teens were racing wave runners. A couple of cousins paddled out in the canoe. A handful fished off the end of the dock. The little kids floated on tubes. Some of us took naps in the hammocks. Others sat around, eating and talking. Who knew that a raging thunderstorm was about to let loose its downpour within seconds of the first sprinkles?

We all raced into the cabin, drenched and smelling like wet puppies, and spent the rest of the evening gathered around the puzzle table or crowded around the television, watching *So You Think You Can Dance* or fixing sandwiches or simply sitting around jawing and cracking each other up.

The next day was more of the same, with the addition of the first-annual Homemade Ice Cream Freeze Off. I found out later than some gung-ho relatives had been fine-tuning their recipes for weeks. The entries ran the gamut. The Nanna Puddin was a five-step process that involved caramelizing bananas, toasting Nilla wafers, and a dash or two of "secret sauce." It won first place. Second place went to the simple, yet always delicious, Fresh Peach. We also sampled Chocolate-Banana, Mint Julep, Vanilla Cookie with Sprinkles, and my entry—Big Red!

I got the recipe from fellow Women of Faith speaker Andy Andrews. It is simple and delicious: seven cans of Big Red soda and one can of condensed milk. That's it. I loved it, but I only won in the Best Color category. (I think the judges made that one up on the spot.) It was a big hit with the kids, but I decided that next time I'll rename it Bubble Gum Sorbet and see if I can satisfy the adult palate.

On the last morning, we sat around the back porch while my stepdad made griddle cakes on the grill. As I looked around at everyone laughing and talking and connecting, I was struck by the wide diversity of stories, even though we all share the same blood.

For instance, there's an adorable couple with a "Broken Road" path to finding each other. They are outgoing, love a good party, enjoy a drink or two, and are delightfully raw, earthy, and real. Then there's another young couple with a completely different lifestyle. She's a preacher's kid, and he's a youth pastor. Their social life revolves around Bible studies, helping single mothers, and mentoring high school kids.

At the other end of the porch, there were relatives who live on twenty acres in the middle-of-nowhere, Texas. They raise cattle (they even won a blue ribbon at the state fair), ride in rodeos, hunt their own meat, make homemade venison jerky, and brought brisket for the weekend that they killed, cleaned, and smoked in their backyard. They were talking to a young couple who had been teased about being "Barbie and Ken." They are the perfect couple, with the perfect house, the perfect child, and the perfect life. And yet, you don't hate them. Everybody loves them.

Mixed into the batch: an uncle with a shotgun, an aunt with chewing tobacco, a single dad, a mother with a baby who has had more than twenty operations, a recent widower, and a great-grandmother caring for her husband with Alzheimer's.

As I watched all the banter and listened to the sharing of hearts and lives, I thanked God for the genius of family. Think about it. Where else would this group of people voluntarily get together and choose to enter each other's lives and accept each other's uniqueness? What an example of God's own family we are!

But I wonder, as Christians, do we really live up to the name "the family of God" that we like to talk about? When I take a survey of my daily life, it doesn't look a whole lot like the back porch of my mother's cabin. Sometimes I exclude some Christian brothers and sisters from my little world because I can't relate to their lives, instead of drawing closer and trying to learn something other than my narrow perspective.

I know that in my everyday life I tend to hang out with a handful of friends who believe the way I do, are at a similar stage of life, and have kids the same ages. For entertainment, we shop at Target, drink coffee at Starbucks, rent Netflix for family night, and download the latest apps on our iPhones.

And yet, I don't see that lifestyle modeled by Jesus. True, he had a dozen friends with whom he chose to hang out the majority of the time, but they were always going new places and meeting different people. He made intentional decisions to encounter the outcasts of Samaria. He dined with Pharisees even though he didn't particularly like their attitudes. He ministered to all kinds of women, whether they were rich, tawdry, depressed, or devoted. His group of guy friends was a mixture of bawdy fishermen, polished tax collectors, Roman officials, and everyday "Joes." His life looked much more like a family model.

Check out the Scriptures. Don't just take my word for it. Jesus hung out with sinners, like you and me. And he didn't try to change them. He loved them. And his love changed them. What is there to change if we're all the same? If I want to influence others with God's love and be changed myself by the power of community, then I may need to be a little more like Jesus, a little more inclusive. I may need to strive to have my circle look a little more like the "family of God" we all talk about.

8

God Can Do Anything

Mary Graham

*God can do anything, you know—far more than you could
ever imagine or guess or request in your wildest dreams!*
—Ephesians 3:20 MSG

I know God can do anything. Of course I do; I've seen
him do more amazing things than I can count. *God can
do anything, you know . . .* it's part of the theme verse for
Women of Faith's *Imagine* events. I hear and/or see those
words just about every day, and I know it's true. But as
much as I hate to admit it, knowing that God *can* doesn't
always mean I expect he *will*.

That being said, I still never walk into the arena on a
Women of Faith weekend without expecting a miracle. At
each event, we hear the sweetest stories of hearts that were
touched and lives that have been changed. I expect that to

happen. I look forward to it. But I never imagined I would hear a story like the one that came to light last year in Dallas.

We look forward to every Women of Faith event, but truthfully, there's something special about the one in Dallas, because it's our own hometown. The Women of Faith office is in Plano, Texas (just north of Dallas), and many of the Porch Pals live in the area. On Dallas weekends many more of our staff attend than is usual in other cities. We even close our call center that Friday so the customer service operators, who spend long days helping others register for our events, can come to be encouraged and renewed themselves.

Every Women of Faith weekend, thousands of women attend events, and it's always profoundly encouraging to know how that can impact a community. However, here in our hometown, we have the possibility of influencing our *own* community, family, church, friends, coworkers, and business leaders. This time there were some twelve thousand women in the American Airlines Center, and we knew many of them personally.

A group from my church in Frisco came. A group from the mall where the Porch Pals often shop came. You may have heard about our friend Sunny, who works at Neiman Marcus and brings dozens of women (and now a couple of men) to the Dallas event each year. Our landscaper came, so he could bring women he felt especially needed the encouragement. Most (if not all) of the women who work in our dental office came. (Their tickets were actually purchased for them by our wonderful dentist.) Even our dog groomer came with her daughters. When you add all the other friends and family members who were there, we were even busier than usual trying to connect with everyone.

Before each event, the emcee (who is frequently—but not always—me) is given a list of the cities and other states from which many attendees come. We call them out from the stage on Saturday, the various groups cheer when their city's name is called, and everyone gets to laugh at my not-always-successful attempts to pronounce the various names. There's no distance award for the person who came the farthest—it's just for fun. Sometimes people have come from really far away to attend Women of Faith—but I don't remember anyone ever coming as far as Meriberi did that weekend.

Road trips of one . . . two . . . even up to four or five hours are common for our attendees. But Meriberi's trip was twenty-two hours *on an airplane*. She lives in New Delhi, India, close to the border of China, and she travelled all that way just to come to Women of Faith. (Now, I might have understood it more easily had she come to visit relatives who live here or to see a doctor for a particular need . . . but just to attend the Women of Faith conference in Dallas?) Needless to say, I was stunned—as was the entire audience.

Meriberi is the youngest of fifteen; her father—who is no longer living—was the first-ever member of his family to become a Christian. Before missionaries arrived in their remote village, Meriberi said her family was "the enemy. We were worshipers of spirits." But her father heard the gospel message and put his faith in Christ regardless of what neighbors or friends might think. He went on to become a pastor and planted many churches. Meriberi herself pastors with her husband. "As young as I am," she told us, "I travel in my own small way in my country to preach and teach the younger women."

Meriberi had been visiting the United States earlier in the year when one of our group leaders told her about Women of Faith. She was interested in the idea, so she went home to New Delhi, did some online research, and decided she just had to be there at the Dallas event. Meriberi explained, "I told my travel agent, 'Book me a ticket.' He said, 'Okay, it will cost this much.'" As it turns out, "this much" was equal to a year-and-a-half's salary. "Until last week," she told me, "I didn't have the money." But God provided—as he always does—and Meriberi was in the audience at *Imagine*.

When I heard this story, I couldn't keep it to myself, so I brought Meriberi up on the stage to share it with everyone in the arena. I don't think it's an exaggeration to say by the time she was finished, there was not a dry eye in the house. The outpouring of love and appreciation from the audience was palpable; she received a standing ovation that seemed to continue forever. Meriberi was a living reminder to us all how blessed we are to have the opportunities we take for granted every day. "Back home," she said, "we never get this kind of privilege to worship. I was just sitting there enjoying every bit of it."

And was the weekend worth all that scrimping and saving and praying and enduring long hours in a plane? Absolutely. In fact, Meriberi shared, "I want to go back and challenge a few more ladies to start saving money, so they can come next year."

Wow. Until I met that sweet woman, the prospect of having a group of women come all the way from India to one of our events was more than I would have asked or imagined. But now that I know Meriberi, I won't be at all surprised when they show up at an arena next year. (At least, I don't think I'll be surprised.)

I wonder . . . how many things do I miss out on, not necessarily because they're "more than I could ever imagine or request" but because I don't bother to imagine, much less request, them? When the travel agent told Meriberi how much a plane ticket to Dallas would cost, it would have been so easy for her to say, "Oh. Well, never mind." After all, who could imagine spending that much money for a weekend women's event? Meriberi could. And she did. Then she requested from her heavenly Father the thing she imagined and started doing what she could to make it happen. And God gave her what she asked.

James 4:2 says "You do not get what you want, because you do not ask God" (NCV). Sometimes, even when I do imagine something, I don't ask for it. Why not? Maybe I just don't think God wants to be bothered with whatever it is I dreamed up. But who knows what he might be able to do with that figment of my imagination? Meriberi probably thought coming to Women of Faith was only about her. "It was the privilege of a lifetime," she said. But the twelve thousand women in the arena that afternoon felt the same way about *hearing* her story—it was the privilege of a lifetime.

She imagined. She asked. She received . . . and so did the rest of us.

What can you imagine?

Maybe God is just waiting for you to ask for it. I've noticed within myself, when my imagination goes to work, it is often on the negative, not the positive. I ask myself these questions: *What if I get sick? What if I run out of money? How in the world could God do that? It's too big to even dream about. What will other people think? How could that happen? It's out of my comfort zone.* But, when we imagine in the positive, our inner wheels start turning, and that sets something into motion that is truly beyond human comprehension. Let your imagination soar—then step out in faith and watch God bring it into reality.

While she was with us, Meriberi said, "I wish you all could come to India and do something like this in our country." Before that weekend, I couldn't imagine such a thing. But now?

God can do anything, you know—far more than you could ever imagine or guess or request in your wildest dreams!

Joy and Laughter

1

Heaven's Funniest Home Videos

. . . .

Mandisa

I love television. I used to be ashamed to admit this so readily, and I always wished I were a more cultured person, enjoying museums and ancient relics. But nope! Give me an episode of *Lost* or *24* over a trip to the Louvre any day! Actually, while my heart will always belong to *24*'s Jack Bauer and the mysterious Smoke Monster from *Lost*, those were only two of the dramas I had committed to (and yes, my heart was broken into pieces when both shows wrapped their final seasons in 2010). But scripted shows aside, I am a reality-TV junkie. I love getting swept up into the tempestuous relationships and broken alliances of *Survivor*. The adrenaline rush from watching teams compete in roadblocks and detours all around the world on *The Amazing Race* is invigorating. And, of course, how can I not mention the pure entertainment of seeing the progression from average Joe to superstar on *American*

Idol? Yes, I recognize that I'm a little obsessed with reality television, but I often wonder if I get a "pass" because I was actually on one!

So far, the only reality show I've ever appeared on is *American Idol*, but I'm certain that one day you will see me on another of my favorite shows. The fact that I sometimes have video cameras aimed in my general direction, combined with my admittedly clumsy nature, makes me a shoo-in to star in my own *America's Funniest Home Video*! I'm just waiting for the day that I trip down the stairs of a stage, do an entire performance with toilet paper hanging out of my dress, or say something really embarrassing on microphone.

Actually, I've already done that.

I'll never forget the first time an audience booed me. I was on the *American Idols Live Tour* in 2006. The producers of the tour chose me to start the show out "with a bang," as they said. Night after night, for sixty concerts, I would take the stage in my shimmering red blouse, glittery eye shadow, and black high heels, singing Chaka Khan's "I'm Every Woman." The sound of the crowd each night was the same: pure, unrestrained excitement! The fact that the majority of the audience was adolescent girls brought the high-pitched screaming to break-point levels! I didn't fool myself into believing those screams were actually for me. I was on tour with Chris Daughtry, Ace Young, Bucky Covington, Elliott Yamin, and Taylor Hicks. Cute boys always elicit a cacophony of squeals, hoots, and shrieks. But at the downbeat of the concert each night, the cute boys were offstage getting their makeup done (yep)! For the first ten minutes of the show, it was all me.

Truth be told, as the lights dimmed and the band played the *American Idol* theme song, the anticipation of the eager crowd would have bubbled over onto whoever took the stage first. As the high-tech doors to the stage flew open and the screams of joy magnified, I would walk the platform, serenading the ladies with the Chaka Khan classic, having an eagle-eye view of women dancing with glee and men fighting hard to maintain their "man cards." As the song came to an end, I would make my way half-way up an ascending ramp, where a microphone stand would be waiting for me. This became the location of my demise.

As the first person onstage, I took it upon myself to thank the audience for their support and to share the appreciation of my fellow tour members for the fans coming that night. By this night in particular, our twenty-third show, we had worked out any kinks and had gotten the hang of things. I made my way up the ramp and waited for the cheers to die down a bit. With all the confidence I could muster I bellowed out, "What's up, Columbus!" It was a bit off-putting not to hear the usual exuberant response. Instead, I heard what sounded like grumbling coming from the crowd of almost twenty thousand people. Then the wave of grumbling turned to full-out booing from this sold-out Columbus crowd! It wasn't until a few awkward moments later that one of the band members got my attention and whispered the words that made my face burn with embarrassment. We were not in Columbus, Ohio. We were in Columbia, South Carolina!

I wish I could say that moments like this have been few and far between. But I've had my share of times when I wished for a rewind button on my life. Still, nothing has been hysterical enough to land me on *America's Funniest Home Videos* quite yet. While I have not been the subject of such a video, I've been present for a few moments when I wished my video camera had been in hand. Like when the Women of Faith worship team was closing out the event with a funky, beat-driven praise song and Luci Swindoll was busting a move on The Porch. Or that time when my band and I arrived in Chicago for a Christmas show and my background singers threw a snowball at my keyboard player, Ronald, causing him to slide to his knees on a frozen puddle of ice. And I think everyone at the 2008 Women of Faith National Conference in San Antonio wished they had a close-up shot when Mary Graham's face turned bright red after Jesus kissed her on the cheek. And by "Jesus," I mean Jim Caviezel, who played the role of Jesus in *The Passion of the Christ*!

I'm pretty sure the real Jesus got a kick out of that one too! As a matter of fact, I think God has a playful side. I mean, have you ever seen a giraffe up close? And then there's one of my favorite stories in Scripture. Acts 20:7–12 is easily overlooked as a laughable situation unless you watch too much *America's Funniest Home Videos,* as I do. I confess that seeing people trip and fall on a weekly basis has had some impact on me. But knowing that the victims of such tumbles are all right from the fact that the video was sent in makes me feel a little better about myself. Similarly, knowing that the subject of this passage of Scripture was okay gives me implied permission to find humor in this story.

Let me set the scene for you. Paul and his fellow travelers had been in Troas for a week. On the last day of their visit, Sunday, they assembled for church. Nothing out of the ordinary so far. Ah, but the story gets better. Apparently because Paul would be leaving the next morning, he had a lot on his mind. I think Luke, the writer of Acts, and I have a lot in common. While most of my fellow artists lean more heavily on the creative side, I tend to be more analytical. Being on time for appointments is important to me. I value promptness. I also value sleep. If I know I need to be up early the next day, a good night of sleep is imperative. I get the feeling Luke felt the same way: "Our plan was to leave first thing in the morning, but Paul talked on, way past midnight" (Acts 20:7 MSG).

Can't you just hear the slight annoyance in that? I imagine that as Paul droned on, Luke and the other believers rolled their eyes and began to sink deeper in their seats. Can't you relate? I have heard thousands of sermons since becoming a Christian in 1992. Most of them were inspiring, eye-opening, even riveting at times. But every now and then, a preacher begins his sermon, then, after an hour, announces that it is time to get to the "meat" now that the introduction is out of the way. I must confess that at times like those I have been known to nod off in my seat. The same thing happened that night in Troas. A young man named Eutychus sat in a window, listening to Paul. Despite the well-lit room in which this little church service was being held, the elapsed time of Paul's preaching was like a dose of Nyquil, and Eutychus began to nod off. In my wild imagination, I can see the congregation glare at their watches as the clock outside the room donged twelve times, indicating that it was midnight. I can hear Paul say (in the Mandisa version of the Bible), "So that's the introduction. Now let's get to the 'meat' of this passage."

Right then, as Eutychus was sinking into what the NIV refers to as "a deep sleep as Paul talked on and on" (Acts 20:9), the attendees jolted alert to the sound of a loud crash! A vase falling from a shelf? No. A table groaning with the fixings of the Lord's Supper? Uh-uh. No, the loud crash was the result of a sound-asleep young man named Eutychus falling out of the window. Can you imagine? Oh, but that is not where it ends. The Bible says that, after falling from a third-story window, Eutychus was "picked up dead" If the story ended there, there would be no humor in this tale. But evidently Paul saved the day: "Paul went down, threw himself on the young man and put his arms around him. 'Don't be alarmed,' he said. 'He's alive!' . . . The people took the young man home alive and were greatly comforted" (vv. 10, 12 NIV).

All is well that ends well, right? I guess Paul learned his lesson about long sermons, huh? Wrong! It seems that after all of the drama of Paul preaching a man to death, the group went upstairs, broke bread, and Paul kept on preaching until daylight! Can you believe it? That story makes me laugh out loud, or LOL as my teen friends would say.

It may just be me, but I'm convinced that God put that story in Acts just for a little comedy break. Whenever I read it, I can almost hear the heavenly chuckles from above laughing along with me. Laughter is a gift from God. It's a package I try to open daily.

God knows how much I love television, so I've asked him for a favor when I finally make it to my heavenly home. I'd like for him to set up a heavenly movie theater room. I anticipate sitting side by side with my Savior as we watch moments in history on a wide, high-definition screen. As we chomp on ooey-gooey, buttered popcorn (with no threat of weight gain—hallelujah!), I would like to see the biblical moments that my imagination doesn't do justice. I envision that viewing the six days of creation will cause me to fall to my knees and worship my Creator. And while Charlton Heston played a great Moses, I would like to see the actual parting of the Red Sea. God will have to bring an entire box of Puffs tissue as we sit, hand in hand, watching Jesus' final moments before the Cross. And when I feel that I can't cry another tear, and God's hands are raw from wiping each one away, I'll ask him to play the scene found in Acts 20. I'll invite Eutychus to join us. You can come too.

2

Still Choosing the Amusing

....

Marilyn Meberg

$\mathcal{J}$ ust because I'm getting older does not mean there are no new things to learn. For example, I have learned how to spell *cataract*, or in my case, *cataracts*. Before my increasingly familiar understanding of the word, I spelled it incorrectly. (Spelling is yet another of my intellectual challenges.) I rarely needed to know how to spell *cataracts*, but in the rare event the need would arise, I jazzed up the spelling by sometimes throwing in an extra *t* or an extra *r* so it appeared as *cattaract*, *catarract*, and on a day in need of special spice, I'd spell it as *cattaracks*.

However, I am learning that cataracts are not to be taken lightly. My need to dignify that noun with its proper spelling has become personal. I do not just have a cataract; I have two of them, thus making me the owner of cataracts.

For those of you yet to own your very own cataracts,

they present an interesting challenge. In essence, they cloud one's vision; what once was clearly defined becomes murky, shadowy, and causes one to mistrust one's visual assumptions.

For example, at one of our Women of Faith events, I was walking toward catering for lunch. We have a designated green room at each of our arenas, where we gather to pray, snack, take off our shoes, or tend to biological needs. I decided to pop into the green room for such a need before going on to lunch.

The room did not appear quite the same as the one I had been in earlier that morning, but the necessities were there even if they didn't look familiar. I was a bit unsettled as big-shoed male feet walked by my stall. I wondered why those feet were there; they are supposed to have their own green room. As I gathered up my purse to leave, I noticed open suitcases scattered all over the floor, with huge tennis shoes, shorts, and shirts spilling out onto the floor. Opening the door for my exit, I squinted at the sign placed there: Crew Room. Well then . . . with that mystery solved, I made my "Mr. Magoo" way to catering for what appeared to be lunch.

I've also learned there is an essential mathematical skill needed to prepare my eyes for cataract removal. Mathematical skills are yet another of my intellectual challenges. The instructions I received are to start three different eyedrops, three times a day, three days before surgery. I was to wait five minutes after administering one kind of drop before putting in another kind. Luci was concerned I would never get this formula right, so she started doing my "drop work." The result: she is exercising her math skills, and we're having unexpected fun time for extra daily chats.

So I have not only learned to spell *cataracts* correctly, I've also learned they have an upside: eyedrop fellowship with my dear friend Luci.

In addition to the fun of eyedrop fellowship with Luci, I've learned the eye-doctor waiting rooms offer unexpected giggle breaks. I have been housed in various waiting rooms on many different occasions, all of which commemorated my progress toward the goal of improved sight. The first visit required drops for eye dilation and then a quiet sit with other persons staring straight ahead while their vision became increasingly murky due to successful dilation.

An elderly gentleman seated next to me in the dilation lineup announced he thought it was too quiet, turned to me, and asked, "How old are you?" I found his question delightfully inappropriate, so I said, "Guess." He trained his good eye on me and said, "Eighty-two." I congratulated him on his one-eyed eyesight and told him I was actually eighty-six. That calculated lie got the whole row involved in speculation. One sweet lady said, "Honey, I may have poor vision at the moment, but you are not a day over eighty." Everyone seemed to agree and settled back into their previous state of silence. Those exchanges were so delicious I could hardly contain myself. I so wanted to stir things up again by saying I am really only seventy-one, but it was just as well I was called out of the lineup to yet another room. As I left them sitting there with their frighteningly enlarged pupils, I said, "See you later." My elderly boyfriend replied, "Don't count on it." I wasn't sure if he had no faith in his ability to see again or if I was too old to be factored into his future.

Not only am I a rotten speller and mathematically challenged, I do not have the gift of calendar. With amazing consistency, I will write down an appointment and then show up at the wrong time or even the wrong day. That has been my maddening pattern for years, and yet each time it happens, I am surprised. "Well, for heaven's sake," I murmur and set off for yet another series of calendar dates that may or may not be accurate and for which I may or may not appear.

This whole cataract experience has been an enormous challenge to my calendar deficit because there are so many appointments. I had been doing fairly well, however, until a week ago. Luci, who will not entrust me to anyone else's care but her own, usually double-checks my appointment book as well as insisting only she can drive me to the eye guy. This is an imposition on her time since the doctor is in Dallas and I'm in Frisco, which is forty minutes (give or take an hour) north of Dallas.

So last week I signed my name and appointment time on the check-in sheet and joined Luci in the midst of people sitting around with varying ocular challenges. There is always something playing on the wide-screen TV. This day was an *I Love Lucy* rerun in which Lucy was stomping grapes at a winery. That's always been one of my favorite reruns, so I was mildly annoyed when I was called over to the appointment desk. "Uhhh . . . I'm sorry Mrs. Meberg, but you don't have an appointment today . . . you are a week early. Your appointment is next week. But you have the day right." "Oh . . . well, for heaven's sake." As I sat back down next to Luci, I didn't have the heart to tell her my mistake until Lucy had finished her grape stomping. "Marilyn, you mean we aren't even supposed to be here today . . . not at all?" "No, honey, I'm due back next week. I am sooo sorry." "No problem, the day is young. Let's do something fun."

Luci and I are never at a loss for conversation, so we set off for Frisco with plans to have lunch at one of our favorite spots. We talked animatedly and nonstop until nothing looked familiar to me. I hated to say anything since I'd lost all credibility and was not even sure my new eyes were to be trusted; I got quiet. Luci seemed unsure of where we were too. Finally I said, "Luci, are we supposed to be on the outskirts of McKinney? Isn't that town quite a bit farther north than even Frisco?" Luci's response was "Should we just keep going? . . . I've never been to McKinney; have you?" It turns out McKinney is a lovely little town with a great restaurant that serves fantastic buttermilk pie. Next time we get lost, we're going back.

The following week, I wrapped up my cataract chapter with my usual aplomb. I checked in at the appointment desk, smiled sweetly, and joined Luci, who was totally absorbed in the movie *Twister* playing on the TV screen. "Marilyn . . . have you ever seen this movie? It is a nailbiter." Within minutes, I joined the waiting-room people in the companionship of nail biting. I was again annoyed as the receptionist called me over to her desk behind the window. "Uhh . . . Mrs. Meberg . . . the good news is you are here on the right day . . . The bad news is you are three hours early." "Uh . . . well, for heaven's sake." I smiled mindlessly and rejoined the nail-biting activity in the waiting room. I didn't have the heart to tell Luci my mistake until the movie was over. Her cheerful response was, "No problem . . . let's get lunch."

As we sat with our salads, I said, "Luci, I have an idea. Since this is my last appointment, what if we just plan on popping into the eye guy's office every Tuesday for the rest of the summer, watch whatever's playing on the wide-screen TV, then wave and leave for lunch. That would totally unsettle the appointment girl. I don't know if I have the heart to do that to her . . . she is so sweet. Of course, I can imagine the stories she has regaled her family with at night: 'You wouldn't believe what that little old gray hair did today . . . bless her heart.'" That plan gave us both a giggle. Three hours later, I was declared "fully sighted" with a well-adjusted new lens in each eye. We haven't yet decided if we want to drive to Dallas next Tuesday for a movie and lunch, but we know it's a delicious option.

Twenty-four years ago, I wrote my first book, entitled *Choosing the Amusing*. The premise of the book is stated in Proverbs 17:22, "A joyful heart is good medicine, but a broken spirit dries up the bones" (NASB). It is my unshakable belief that if we can find humor in our circumstances, it will keep us from a broken heart and dry bones. While some circumstances are so overwhelming that we have to search hard for even a shred of humor, once we find it, medicine is applied to our hurt.

I have no hesitation in admitting I have a narrow band of competence. I have made my living within that narrow band. I can teach, speak, write, and "shrink." Jobs that require more than what my narrow band has to offer must go to someone else. In the meantime, I am free to do what I love to do, botch up what I can't do, and in it all, find myself choosing the amusing. If you'd like, I'd love to have you join me. Write Luci for directions.

3

Making Sad Faces Happy

....

Patsy Clairmont

Watch out! I'm cranky today, and it ain't pretty. I know because I passed a mirror and almost scared myself when I caught a glimpse of my scowling face. Oh my. With all my maturity lines, my scowls have taken on a new dimension . . . like a menopausal Shar-Pei. (Well, I have been known to bark, growl, and even bite occasionally.)

I hate it when I'm this way. I want to shape up, but the least annoyance seems magnified inside my firecracker emotions. I had a talk with me, but I'm not sure I was paying attention because my husband said something fairly innocuous to me and I snarled my answer at him. Poor guy. He didn't deserve that.

That's the problem with bad moods . . . they tend to lash out at innocent bystanders. That saying "If mama ain't happy, ain't nobody happy" is obviously the result of someone's firsthand experience. (I suspect that "someone" may be a member of my family.) Crotchety loves company. After all, why should others be perky when I'm prickly? I know, I know, it's not very nice and probably not very smart either. The psalmist knew what he was talking about when he wrote, "When my heart was sad and I was angry, I was senseless and stupid" (Psalm 73:21–22 NCV). I'd like to hear the story behind that one, wouldn't you?

I need to be alone . . . on a deserted island. Then if I decided to act up I'd be the only one affected. But quite honestly, I'm not even enjoying my own company. I tried being stern with myself ("Shape up, Clairmont!"), but it only made me angry. I'm not fond of stern people . . . even if they are related.

I tried going for a walk, but it was hot, and sweat makes me cantankerous. And who needs cranky, layered with snarling, seasoned with cantankerous? That's a bad casserole any way you mix it. I mean, who'd knowingly volunteer to show up for dinner if that was on the menu?

Speaking of menu, at one point I drifted into the kitchen and began feeding my bad mood. Who needs a deserted island when you can have a "desserted" island instead? (Kitchen island, that is.) I've learned that bad moods—my bad moods, anyway—don't much care for healthy options. They demand chocolate. So I gave my bad mood a little . . . well, maybe more than a little. (One pan of brownies equals one serving, doesn't it?) Bad decision—it only added guilt to my whiny repertoire.

When it comes to a dish of cantankerousness, guilt is often one of the major ingredients. We feel guilty about something, and rather than doing something that would actually help (like fessing up and asking forgiveness), we take out our bad feelings on those around us. Which just gives us more to feel guilty about, which leads to more snarling, which leads to . . . you get the picture.

Old wounds are another flavor in many cranky pies. There's a hurt hiding in a corner of our heart, and every so often it flares up. We could deal with it, but that might not be pleasant, so . . . nah, let's just stuff it back down. Trouble is, that leaves us uncomfortable and, well, cranky.

Sometimes we try to ignore our inner mess and hope it'll go away while we're not looking. When I spotted some turtles sunning themselves at the edge of the pond, I hurried out to greet them in hopes of finding an entertaining distraction from my sorry self. But before I could even get close, they ducked into the water and paddled away as fast as their little turtle legs could carry them. It was like they'd all gotten the memo: "If you think *your* shell is hard, wait until you meet this one!"

I do sometimes resemble a turtle . . . I've been known to retreat into my shell, only coming out to snap at the ones closest to me before diving back under cover. (Or under the covers.) That kind of shell generally forms over those wounds I mentioned earlier. No matter how firmly we stuff them down, there's always a chance that anyone who gets too close may find them and make things worse, so we put on armor to keep people away. Problem is, a shell works great at keeping things out, but it can get lonely in there. Trust me, I know.

Plus, left unchecked, what started out as a protective coating eventually results in what the Bible calls a "hard heart." And hard hearts lead to nothing but grief.

Proverbs 28:14 in the New King James Version says, "He who hardens his heart will fall into calamity." Now, I'm a big fan of cowgirls, but I sure don't want to turn into Calamity Patsy. I looked up that verse in a different version to see if I liked it any better, but things just got worse. Look at this, the same verse from the New Century Version: "Those who are stubborn will get into trouble." Stubborn! I'm not stubborn; I'm determined. Why, I'll show you who's . . . uh-oh, is that a shell starting to form? What was that description from Psalm 73? "Senseless and stupid"? Humph.

Here's another problem with shells: just when you think you're safe, something (or someone) comes along and kicks you over. Have you ever seen upside-down turtles? The poor things lie there, kicking their little arms and legs for all they're worth, going nowhere. (Ever been there?) They're stuck until someone comes along to rescue them. Meanwhile their vulnerable parts are laid open to the sun. (Or in the case of us human turtles, the Son.)

Here's what surprises me . . . not that I'm difficult (I learned that a long time ago) but that God isn't taken aback by my behavior. Now, don't misunderstand—I'm not saying he approves of my crabby attitude, but he already knows I'm capable, not just of crabby, but of much, much worse. That's why he made provision for me (and you) at Calvary.

So here's what I'm going to do, and you can join me if you need to: I'm going to get down on my knobby knees and ask Christ to rescue me from myself yet again. To change my contrary heart. To forgive my indulgent behavior. Then I'm going to get up and deliberately go ask my husband to forgive me . . . yet again. Finally, I'm going to take a walk and bask in my sweaty glow.

Who knows, maybe I'll have gained a grain of wisdom through all this. That would be good for my scowling Shar-Pei countenance. It says so in Ecclesiastes 8:1: Wisdom brings happiness; it makes sad faces happy.

Here's to happier faces and a better day!

4

So You Think You Can't Dance

. . . .

Lisa Harper

One of my favorite Bible stories depicting joy takes place when the Israelites finally get to bring the ark of the covenant back to Jerusalem after it had been missing for a long time. (The ark of the covenant is the golden box that contained holy relics—like the stone tablets on which were inscribed the Ten Commandments or a jar of manna—symbolizing God's affection for and commitment to his people.) According to Samuel, this was actually the second time King David had attempted to bring the priceless box home because the first attempt ended in disaster when some of his buddies ignored one of God's "ark transport" rules. Which means the subsequent march toward Jerusalem was a very slow, careful procession . . . that is, until David realized they're just a few feet away from the finish line and he couldn't bottle his bliss any longer: "And David danced before the LORD with all his might. And David was wearing a linen ephod. So David and all the house of Israel brought up the ark of the LORD with shouting and with the sound of the horn" (2 Samuel 6:14–15 ESV).

David didn't care if people watching the Ark Parade thought he was crazy. He didn't mind if they thought twirling was inappropriate behavior for a monarch. He even ignored his wife Michal's grumpy, "This is probably going to be an embarrassing clip on YouTube" glare. The shepherd boy who became a king simply couldn't contain his delight over God's goodness!

Several years ago, I met someone whose unbridled joy reminds me of David. A friend had asked if I would be one of the speakers at the inaugural conference for a faith-based addiction recovery program her brother was starting. She said the audience was going to be made up mostly of people who were earnestly trying to break free from the choke hold of alcoholism, drug abuse, and various sexual addictions. Although I haven't struggled with those particular issues, I told her I'd be honored to come and would probably fit right in since I was a recovering Pharisee, desperate for God's mercy too. And my assumption was correct because, when the event started one Friday night several months later, I found myself looking at the men and women around me—most with nicotine stains on their fingers and expectancy etched on their faces—and thought, *This is definitely my tribe!*

I also found myself quickly intrigued by a woman on the front row who danced throughout the entire opening worship set. Her outfit was more vintage than hip, and her long hair was streaked with gray, but her upturned face radiated pure joy. Much like King David during his boogie fever episode, she seemed totally unaware—or at least unconcerned—that anyone might be judging her while she swayed and dipped and spun. I mused, *I bet there's some amazing story behind why she dances like that.*

I was thrilled early the next morning when I walked into the church where the conference was taking place and saw her praying at the altar by herself. When she got up, I walked over and introduced myself and told her how much I had appreciated her carefree expression of worship the night before. She seemed a little embarrassed, but mostly pleased, by the attention and told me her name was Joyce. She went on to tell me the short version of how God saved her from a nightmarish existence of booze and bad men.

I could've listened to her all day long—not just because her story was so redemptive but because of the way she told it in a distinctive, gravelly, baritone voice. I hugged her hard when the emcee walked toward the podium to begin the morning session, and I whispered, "I hope we have more time to talk today!" before scurrying to my seat.

A little while later I got to address the group, and because I like to be as close as possible to the audience when teaching, I walked down the sanctuary steps during the opening illustration. And then, right when I was about to read the passage from Hebrews we were focusing on, I looked down and realized I was standing directly in front of Joyce. So I proudly announced, "This is my new friend, Joyce. She's got an awesome voice, and she's going to read the text for us!"

Now, I don't normally bombard strangers with requests to speak in public; I don't even ask friends in our weekly Bible study to read out loud unless I've cleared it with them ahead of time. But for some reason, in that moment, I felt compelled to have Joyce read. I handed her my Bible—which was open to the selected passage—and held the microphone up to her mouth while she recited the verses. She stumbled over a few hard words but didn't seem nervous. We grinned at each other when she finished, and everyone clapped politely; then she sat down, and I continued teaching.

When the conference was over, Joyce approached me at the back of the room and said, "I need to talk to you about what happened when you asked me to read this morning." I thought, *Oh no, now I've done it! She's probably one of those people who abhors talking in front of a group, and I've really offended her.* Joyce paused before confessing softly, "When I told you Jesus saved me from alcoholism, I didn't tell you I fell off the wagon eight months ago and got rip-roaring drunk after thirteen years of sobriety." She explained how she'd turned briefly back to liquor for one night after finding out the man she was engaged to had betrayed her and taken up with another woman.

She added, "I know you didn't know this church (where the conference was held) kicked me off the leadership team after I confessed my mistake." Joyce went on to express how painful the dismissal had been, and although she didn't blame them for the consequences of her bad choices, she still felt as if she were wearing a scarlet letter A for *alcoholic* every time she entered the sanctuary afterward. She eventually left that congregation and joined another church across town because she couldn't quite get past the humiliation she'd experienced there.

I said, "Joyce, I'm so sorry." She held up her hand and said, "Wait, there's more. There's also no way you could've known that reading in public has always terrified me. I don't know my dad—he left before I was born—and my mom was still basically a kid herself when she got pregnant. She dropped out of school in the ninth grade and never finished her education. Mama did her best, but she didn't know how to teach me the basics of reading and writing before I started school myself."

Then Joyce told me that, on her very first day of elementary school, a naive young teacher called on her to read out loud. She described standing up in front of the class with her knees knocking and hands trembling and how she desperately tried to make sense out of the black and white symbols swimming on the pages of her book. When she stuttered and made up a phrase she hoped was close to what was written, the other children laughed and called her stupid. She said from that day forward if she ever had to read in front of anyone in school or at work, she'd study the required "speech" for weeks ahead of time and struggle with anxiety until the ordeal was over.

She smiled at my open-mouthed response and concluded with sparkling eyes, "This weekend is the first time I've been in this building since I left in shame, but today felt like my coming-out party. This place of disgrace became a place of honor because out of all these people, you picked *me*. It's like the Lord was saying, 'That's my girl!' in front of everybody!"

After a few seconds of stunned awe, we both started giggling like teenagers over the sweet stunt God had obviously pulled on her behalf. And my vocabulary is far too small to capture the glory of our encore routine. "She is clothed with strength and dignity; she can laugh at the days to come" (Proverbs 31:25 NIV).

5

Why Be Happy When You Can Own a Home?

. . . .

Luci Swindoll

Which is worse: hearing an explosion in your house or having the house move from here to there of its own free will? Both actually happened this year. Even though my house is relatively new, it seems to have a mind of its own and apparently packs up and moves—on its own.

The explosion happened at midnight on March 9, 2010. I heard the sound coming from somewhere in my house and thought, *What in the world was that? I think the chimney fell in.* I was on my way to bed, so I grabbed a flashlight and headed toward the living room, then the kitchen, then the utility room . . . all the while moving slowly toward the front of the house . . . turning on lights as I went and listening carefully to determine what had happened. By the time I got to the refrigerator, I heard a splashing noise coming from the garage. (Trust me! You never want to hear splashing *anywhere* in the middle of the night!) Once I walked through the door that leads to my garage, I saw water *streaming* from the opening where the attic ladder is stored and bouncing off the cement floor. *Oh. My. Gosh.* I said to myself. *Should I open that trap door and run the chance of drowning?* The answer came quickly: *YES, you moron. Open it. Don't just stand there.* Immediately I climbed the ladder, looked into the attic, and shined the flashlight on the water heater, wondering if it had burst. It didn't look like it, but the ceiling of the garage (under the heater) was wet and getting wetter by the minute.

(Parenthetically, picture this: there were stacked cardboard boxes in the garage that held dozens of little stuffed birds and bird nests I had used for decorations at a birthday party a few months before. Of course, those boxes had gotten soaked and fallen over, and there were birds *everywhere*. At first glance, they looked like they were trying to swim to an unknown shore with their nests in tow. And here I was, in my pajamas, soaking wet, tramping around on the cement floor barefooted, hardly able to catch my breath from laughing . . . picking up wet birds. Such wonderful incongruity. I loved it.)

You have to understand, when one lives alone and is self-sufficient, an explosion with a subsequent water problem epitomizes *the acid test*. Amazingly, I was not only tickled but also very calm (inherited traits from my father) and analyzed the situation this way:

1. I don't know how to turn off the water.
2. Since there was an explosion, the pressure's off.
3. I'll call a plumber in the morning.
4. I need to trust the Lord with the outcome.

Looking at all those facts in my mind and agreeing with them, I did the next best thing. I went to bed. (I know. I can't believe it either. Call me Noah.) At 7 a.m., I awakened, threw on my jeans, called a friend who's a builder, and in no time he came and confirmed my suspicions. The water heater was indeed the culprit. It had burst and given forth a fountain that had run down onto the cement, under the garage door, down the driveway, into the gutter, and on the street for six or seven hours. I now had a virtual swimming pool, albeit an inch deep and a mile wide. *But you picked up the birds, Luci*, I thought to myself. *No one knows you had an aviary in here last night. Remember that enjoyable moment?*

I called a plumber to replace the water heater, a drying service to dry the ceiling (this took four days), the city inspector to okay the installment, and my insurance company to submit a claim. All in all, it was about a week's worth of getting things back to normal. The story is recorded in my journal and etched in my mind, and I thank God every day that I didn't panic and that he stopped the water flow before it seeped into my house and did terrible damage.

But then, four months later *this* happened. My house started sinking. Well, actually it had been *trying* to sink for several months, but this is when I first noticed it. I live in Texas in an area of clay composite soil. The house, built in 2004, sits on a concrete slab foundation, and when there's movement of the soil, the slab goes with it, causing stress on various parts of the building—outside on the bricks, inside on the walls, and underneath on the foundation. I didn't feel the house moving, but I saw evidence of it around me. Upon investigation, John (my builder friend who rescued me from the water heater problem) told me the house needed "jacking up," like you'd jack up a car to remove a flat tire. I found it all so interesting but seemingly impossible to imagine. "You can do that to a house?" I asked.

"Oh yeah," John said. "People do it all the time."

Well, you coulda fooled me.

An engineer came to do a "foundation investigation," and based on his report, I hired a reputable company to come out, dig holes in twelve places around the back and side of the house where it was sinking, insert metal piers fifteen feet deep, and move the house back to its proper dwelling place. Within eight hours and with the work of twelve men with lots of equipment, my house became level once again. Who knew? During their time here, John came to supervise the work, and I invited neighborhood friends to come over and watch. John's wife also came to keep me company. My Women of Faith buddies gathered around for moral support, and the diggers came to do the work. They were all listening to the World Cup on the radio as they worked—happy as clams. They, no doubt, jack up houses every day, so they were laughing and yelling and having a party. They were the pros, and I was the happy home owner.

Everything in me knows I could have lost so much more than a few days of inconvenience, a few moments of concern, and a couple hours of sleep when my water heater exploded. In reality, I could have lost my house and its treasures that are irreplaceable and precious to me. And there's no guarantee I won't lose all that in the future. I know people who have lost material possessions and loved ones in all kinds of horrific circumstances.

And I'm well aware of the fact that my "mobile home" could have suffered much more damage than it did. Or I could have been slapped with a repair bill I was unable to pay. I know all that and am fully aware of the fact that God was with me in these moments of testing. It is God who kept me sane. It is God who enabled me to laugh. It is God who gave me the money to pay for my house to be put back together. And, most important, it is God who helped me find joy in the middle of the difficulty on both counts.

But here's the secret of why I can be happy and own a home: I gave this house to God when it was built in 2004. I wrote that desire in my mind and heart. And I wrote it in stone. One rainy night, I came to the site and wrote in the wet cement (which is now under a garage wall): *This house is dedicated to God. 04-07-04. L. Swindoll.* Every time something goes haywire in it, I remind myself that it's God's house—I'm only the caretaker here. Let me tell you, that fact has made *all* the difference. There's something freeing in one's spirit when we give back to God what he's given us in the first place. It creates a different attitude than thinking, *I own this. It's mine!* Knowing that and reminding myself of it every day enables me to stay calm when things go wrong and laugh about what I simply don't understand. And I can write about it with a smile on my face. The verses of Psalm 9:1–2 in *The Message* express it best: "I'm thanking you, God, from a full heart, I'm writing the book on your wonders. I'm whistling, laughing, and jumping for joy; I'm singing your song, High God."

We can trust a God we know is there, although we don't see him. He may not do what we want, but he always does what's best. And God works everything together for our good. For example, all my loved ones have now had their hot water heaters replaced with new ones, and they've written down the name of the engineer who inspected my foundation, just in case their homes decide to go south for the winter.

6

The Power of Friendship

....

Mary Graham

Friends are huge in the overall scheme of things. Even Jesus had friends when he walked on the earth. And, Jesus calls *us* his friends. He places a high premium on friendship.

So do I. Perhaps it's because my mother modeled it. She had a very close circle of friends I still remember from the hours and days they spent hanging out at our house—visiting, laughing, and drinking iced tea. I remember the days I would see my mother in the kitchen, baking a pie or a "hot dish" to take to a friend's home because someone was not well or had lost a loved one.

My sisters (I had four older ones) had friends I loved. I would sneak around to hear them talking, so I would have something interesting to say when the time came. (We won't mention how many times I got in big trouble for telling something, as my mother said, "out of turn.")

My brothers (I had three older ones) had company all the time. I remember seeing one of them after we became adults when I was visiting our old neighborhood. I was trying to place who he was and how I knew him when he said to me, "Don't you remember I lived at your house for a year? I wasn't getting along at home and your brother told me I could live with your family. I'm not sure your mother ever knew that. She might've thought I was just there a lot."

Growing up we had relatives who lived several states away. They always came to visit, and we sat on the porch, listening to them telling stories and laughing constantly. Having people around was in our DNA. We weren't always invited to other people's homes (there were way too many of us), but we always had an abundance of people at our house.

Now that I'm an adult and have a home of my own, it doesn't surprise me that friends hang out at my house. I've shared a home with my friend Ney Bailey for many years. In the early years of our living together, we worked on the same ministry team and each of us traveled a good bit in our work, although we rarely traveled together. In time, Ney began to realize that I often invited people to stay with us, or even live with us, without mentioning it to her. One day, she said to me, "Mary, if someone needs a place to stay, I have no problem with her staying with us. But, please. Let's talk about it first just to be sure I've not made some other plan." I thought that seemed weird at the time, but I tried to remember. (And now I can laugh at my insensitivity.)

The disciples lived and worked together. They enjoyed companionship, and they helped one another grow in faith and faithfulness. And to this day, God calls us to work together, grow together, and "stimulate one another to love and good deeds" (Hebrews 10:24 NASB).

One of the greatest blessings of Women of Faith is that we are a community. We share the same faith, trust the same God, desire the same ministry, and grow together as friends and disciples. Several years ago, after I had lived in Texas a couple years, I said to my longtime friends Luci and Marilyn at the Dallas airport as they were changing planes to fly to their respective homes in California, "If you lived here, you'd be home now." I don't remember how they responded that first time, but I remember repeating that phrase a few dozen times thereafter.

Finally, one day Luci was staying with me in Texas and started to inquire about building a house here. She found a lot near us and fulfilled her lifelong dream of designing and building a home with a huge library for her book collection. It wasn't long until Marilyn did the same. At first she only stayed in the summer months, but out of the blue, she decided to move into our neighborhood. A few years before Luci and Marilyn came, we got a call from Barry Walsh. He asked if he and Christian could spend a few days with us before Christian's school started and while Sheila was writing a book. They were with us a couple days, and I'm not sure how it happened, but we started looking for a home for them and a school for Christian. For several years, Patsy and Les Clairmont spent a few months every year in Frisco to escape the Michigan winters. We even had Nicole Johnson down the street from Marilyn for a few years. She never lived here full-time, but we always considered her our neighbor.

We all love our church, our neighborhood, and the community, and we especially love flying in and out of Dallas, which makes all our weekend travel so much easier. Living in the same neighborhood isn't the secret, however. It's the community. I remember one night in particular (although there are thousands of similar examples). During the Thanksgiving weekend, when Patsy was in town for a wedding, we encouraged her to find a house in the neighborhood for the winter. After church on Sunday, Patsy and I decided to do just that. While we were looking, Luci phoned me to let me know that Ney (who wasn't feeling well that morning) had gotten very sick, and she was taking Ney to the emergency room. She wanted us to know so we could pray.

We prayed, but we also drove straight to the hospital. As we entered the waiting area, it was full of people we know—Barry, Sheila, Marilyn, Luci, and a few others. When we found out that Ney needed a few prescriptions filled for treatment, Barry headed for the pharmacy, Sheila headed out to buy dinner for everyone, Luci brought Ney home, and Patsy and I followed them. In time we found ourselves sitting around the table. Ney was taken care of, we had eaten dinner, and now we could look through brochures to find a house for Patsy and Les.

That evening wasn't all that unusual. Quite honestly, it's the way we live. If someone is sick, or in need, or has good news or bad, we gather 'round. We care about one another, we help each other, and we learn and grow together. Actually, it seems completely right to me.

Certainly there is a convenience about our being together. We use the same handyman and gardener. We go to the same grocery store and share rides to the airport. We are a community who celebrates life together and takes care of one another. We learn and grow together, and we work out our differences as necessary.

The most important part of our community and the thing that means the most in the overall scheme of things is that none of this is about us. It's actually about our calling. God put us together as a team. Even though we have different gifts, talents, and interests, we work at having harmony and love during those times when it doesn't come naturally or easily. We learn to be honest with each other, and we practice forgiveness. We help each other grow and speak the truth in love to one another. We bear one another's burdens and pray for each other's needs. We laugh together—and cry together. We give to each other, challenge each other, and share the good, the bad, and the ugly parts of our lives together. We simply enjoy one another.

Because that's what we've learned from knowing how Jesus lived with his disciples, it's what we're committed to in our relationships and in the ministry of Women of Faith. The question I'm often asked is, what is it like to be in this circle of friends? To tell the truth, it's very much like being at a Women of Faith weekend.

About four million women have attended Women of Faith events in the past fifteen years. Many of them have come in groups of ten or more. Women attend in family groups, neighborhood groups, groups of people who work together, and church groups. It's not unusual for someone to introduce me to others in the group by saying, "This is our Porch." Women write to say they've become closer in their own friendships having enjoyed the conference as a group. When I go to my hotel room on a Friday night, I often walk past open doors with women sitting all around, even on the floor, laughing and talking. And I think, *That's like us.*

It is not good for man (or woman, I might add) to be alone. We need each other. And we need to care for one another. Don't miss it.

7

Catch That Train

. . . .

Lisa Whelchel

> *"So I have come down to deliver them out of the hand of the*
> *Egyptians, and to bring them up from that land to a good*
> *and large land, to a land flowing with milk and honey."*
>
> —Exodus 3:8 NKJV

Sounds like God invited the children of Israel to join him on a fabulous trip to the promised land, doesn't it? Since we have the benefit of knowing the beginning, middle, and end of that story, we know the journey didn't go quite as they may have planned. We also know that, even though it was a much harder and longer route than they anticipated, it was more than worth the exhaustingly circuitous way of getting there.

Often it would be nice to know the end of the story while we're in the midst of it. But God just doesn't work that way—as I've found time and time again. A two-day, twenty-nine-mile, leisurely biking getaway proved that to me. It started with my mom asking—out of the blue—would I like to go with her on a weekend bike trip in Vermont. The next weekend. I don't own a bike, and the last time I even rode one was probably sometime before I had children, but I remembered what my beloved grandmother, "Nanny," always told me: "Catch that train while you can because you never know if it will pass this way again."

The brochure said that we would be biking twelve miles the first day and seventeen miles the second day. We realized we'd better get training before we flew to New England on the following Friday. On Monday, we rode the stationary bike for six miles. On Tuesday, we rode real bikes for six miles. On Wednesday, we bought bike shirts, socks, and shorts. On Thursday, we biked in our neighborhood another six miles. That was the extent of our training.

We packed up our new bike clothes, along with our naivete, and headed for our weekend destination, a quaint bed-and-breakfast in the middle of Vermont. We were especially excited about the chef's reputation for gourmet cooking. We arrived just as they were serving the first course of dinner. I must confess, we were a bit surprised when my mom was served her entrée. When we had called for directions from the airport, the innkeeper had asked us which of the four entrées we would like for dinner. I had chosen chicken, and my mom had chosen the chili and sea bass. (That sounded really good on this crisp, cool fall evening.) By the time my mom was served her chocolate ganache cheesecake, we realized she wasn't going to get her bowl of chili. We later figured out she had ordered Chilean sea bass. Oops.

The next big surprise was meeting the group we would be riding with for the next two days. They were young. They were fit. They had brought their own professional bikes and gear—and they obviously knew what they were doing. Uh-oh. This was our first indication we were maybe not on a straight line to the promised land. My mom affectionately dubbed them "The Kennedys." They talked of vacationing at their island home and parties at the lake house and grandparents who had letters from the president. And we were at the other end of the table still waiting for a bowl of chili.

After dinner, we met with our adorable tour guide, Michelle. Now, picture your favorite camp counselor, imagine her spending her life biking, hiking, cross-country snowshoeing, helicopter-dropped skiing, and eating granola she made herself, and you get the picture. This girl knew the outdoors intimately.

We took a seat in the billiard room to go over the bike route for the next day. Michelle passed out the maps. For the first day of biking, the shortest distance planned was a twenty-two-mile loop, but everyone quickly agreed that the forty-four-mile loop to Woodstock and back was the way to go, with the possibility of an additional twenty-mile hill-climbing option if everyone felt up for it. Oops again.

Neither one of us had ever ridden farther than six miles, and we were just praying we could make it the twelve miles advertised on the website for the first day's route. I sent a text message to my friend Priscilla asking her to pray for rain.

The next morning we awoke to rain. Praise the Lord! We were spared. Or so we thought. But, no! They were planning to ride in the rain. We had no choice; we had to play along. Mom and I put on our helmets (backwards), made it the first five miles, and were graciously met by Michelle at the bottom of "Hysteria Hill." She offered to load up our bikes and drive us to the top. "Yeah, thanks. In this rain, I just don't know if we could make it." (I didn't mention the fact that we couldn't have made that hill on electric bikes.)

However, the rest of the day was idyllic. We stopped at the Calvin Coolidge birthplace and memorial. We drank his favorite soda, Moxie, and ate maple syrup cotton candy. We taste-tested Vermont cheddar cheese and bought souvenirs. Once again, Michelle came to our rescue by driving up with the van just about the time we remembered that we were traveling on bicycles and had just bought another five pounds to stuff into our little bike bags.

Mom and I finally arrived in Woodstock. The rest of the team had already come and gone and were halfway up the optional hill-climbing route. We didn't care. We had just ridden ten miles farther than either one of us ever dreamed we would.

The next morning we woke up thankful that the sky was clear so we could ride the entire twenty-five-mile trip. We got an early start and especially enjoyed the day's route with lots of back roads and beautiful covered bridges. I strapped on my iPod, popped in one earplug, and set my playlist to my favorite motion picture soundtracks. I imagined myself in a slow-motion montage, riding through the fall foliage, with soaring music scoring my journey.

Later in the day, I selected Josh Groban and had a spiritual experience all in itself as my front wheel barreled through freshly fallen orange, red, purple, and yellow leaves. I'm not kidding you; just as Josh and Charlotte Church crescendoed in their duet, "The Prayer," a strong breeze swept through the trees, and leaves start swirling from everywhere. It felt as if I were in the middle of a snow globe, except I was surrounded by beautiful leaves. And I can't even begin to express the overwhelming feeling of worship I experienced when I tuned my iPod to CeCe Winans's "Throne Room" while riding through the middle of God's masterpiece of beauty in the fall foliage of New England.

I hate to think what I might have missed had we not

impulsively decided to do something we'd never done before. Or if we'd been daunted by the fact that we didn't have all the right training or equipment. Or if we'd given up when we learned that the journey would be longer and harder than we anticipated.

This wasn't the first journey in my life when I truly didn't think I could make it to the end. And I've certainly grumbled before like the children of Israel. But I learned that God was the one who set me on the path; he promised to go with me, and he would bring me to the destiny he planned for me from the beginning. I want to have the same attitude about these harder life journeys as my Nanny had about her life: to hop on that train. I'm sure God has something good planned!

8

Where Is the Joy in Pain and Suffering?

. . . .

Sheila Walsh

*Sing to the LORD a new song, for he has done
marvelous things; his right hand and his holy arm
have worked salvation for him.*

—Psalm 98:1 NIV

*D*epending on the biblical translation you use, the word *joy* is included in about thirty-five of the one hundred and fifty psalms of the Old Testament. You are probably familiar with that reality. We associate David with his call for us to praise God, to be joyful in his presence:

"Sing joyfully to the LORD, you righteous; it is fitting for the upright to praise him." (Psalm 33:1 NIV)

"Clap your hands, all you nations; shout to God with cries of joy! How awesome is the Lord Most High, the great King over all the earth!" (Psalm 47:1–2 NIV)

"Shout with joy to God, all the earth! Sing the glory of his name; make his praise glorious! Say to God, 'How awesome are your deeds! So great is your power that your enemies cringe before you.'" (Psalm 66:1–3 NIV).

But what I found most compelling as I studied each one of those psalms again is that many of the psalms that speak of joy don't start there. They start with pain or struggle or even doubt and end with David's personal experience of joy and a call to us to be joyful. Look at Psalm 28 for example: "To you I call, O Lord my Rock; do not turn a deaf ear to me. For if you remain silent, I will be like those who have gone down to the pit. Hear my cry for mercy as I call to you for help, as I lift up my hands toward your Most Holy Place" (vv. 1–2 NIV).

This psalm of David is known as a psalm of lament. It seems from these first few verses that David is experiencing what many of us experience at times, the silence of God. Have you ever been there? Perhaps you find yourself there at this moment? We all go through seasons when God doesn't seem very close. We pray and ask him to answer, and sometimes the intimacy that we have known before seems to have vanished.

In this psalm, David is doing all he knows to do, crying out for mercy, lifting his hands in worship, reminding God that without his presence he has no hope. David's honesty with our Father is a refreshing challenge to me. He doesn't pretend to "feel" spiritual or close to God; he simply pours his heart out. It seems as if that very transparent intimacy makes way for joy.

As the psalm continues, we read these words, "Praise be to the LORD, for he has heard my cry for mercy. The LORD is my strength and my shield; my heart trusts in him, and I am helped. My heart leaps for joy and I will give thanks to him in song" (vv. 6–7 NIV).

I wonder why it is that we are afraid to be honest with God about the depths of our emotions. Is it that we don't want to admit that he seems distant, or is it that it seems wrong somehow to question God? It may be that it feels disrespectful to be openly angry with our Father. But I believe that honesty in every area of life is a hallmark of true relationship and indicates a depth of trust. I will never forget the process of watching my then four-year-old son, Christian, process his emotions after the death of his beloved papa. William had lived with us for two years after the death of my mother-in-law, and he and Christian were buddies. The night William died of a heart attack, Christian and I were the only ones home with him. We watched as the paramedics worked on William at our home, and we then followed the ambulance to the hospital. But by the time we arrived, William had died.

I watched Christian carefully in the days and weeks that followed and saw what I anticipated, his obvious grief as he mourned the loss of someone he loved so much. But then one day I saw something surprising. I was in the kitchen and watched as Christian pushed our cat, Lily, off the edge of the sofa in our den. This was very uncharacteristic of my son. Christian loved Lily, plus he wasn't ever rough with animals. I suggested to him that we might go for a walk. As we walked alongside the golf course that bordered our home, I asked him if he was angry, and he admitted that he was.

"You told me, Mom, that God hears and answers my prayers," he said. "Well, when we were following the ambulance to the hospital, I asked him not to take my papa, and he did anyway. I don't understand, and I'm not going to pray anymore."

How I understood his pain and confusion. Which one of us has not found ourselves in that place where we just don't understand why God didn't answer our prayers the way we pleaded that he would? We walked home, and I took Christian to a sports store, where I purchased boxing gloves and a punching bag. When we had it all set up, I told him that God is big enough and loves us enough to allow us to be angry.

"When you find yourself so angry and upset that you

don't know what to do, put on your gloves and hit this bag as hard as you can," I said. "It's okay to be mad; you just can't hurt yourself or anyone else. And when you've poured it all out, God will be waiting to hold you."

I think that when we block one emotion, we hamper them all. When we push anger or disappointment or fear into the basement of our lives and slam the door closed, we cast a long shadow over joy as well. But when we understand that God knows our frailty and longs to embrace us just where we are, that gives us freedom to bring all of who we are to him.

David certainly knew that to be true. After he had committed adultery with Bathsheba and participated in sending her husband to his certain death, he took his shame and guilt and bitter regret to God. As one of the most heartfelt, poignant psalms, David's prayer has led thousands and thousands over the centuries from places of darkness back to a place of true joy that comes from knowing that we are known and we are loved:

> Create in me a pure heart, O God, and renew a steadfast spirit within me. Do not cast me from your presence or take your Holy Spirit from me. Restore to me the joy of your salvation and grant me a willing spirit, to sustain me. Then I will teach transgressors your ways, and sinners will turn back to you." (Psalm 51:10–13 NIV)

If you find your life a little lacking in joy today, ask God to show you if you have pushed some of your feelings so far down inside that they dragged joy with them. Joy is your birthright as a daughter of God.

Comfort

1

The Loving Touch

. . . .

Marilyn Meberg

I remember the flurry of words that engulfed presidential candidate Barack Obama and his wife, Michelle, when they did a fist bump concluding a campaign speech. That fist bump created inordinate commentary from television talking heads and newspaper writers. I thought, *Mercy . . . how hard up is the media for issues worthy of discussion?*

However, that fist bump commentary inspired me to do a pleasant little meander down my own nonmedia ponder path. That path is often strewn with confusing and overgrown plant life in need of pruning, but some opinions come to light that I agree with. (Sometimes I don't agree with what I think I think, but that's another subject.) Here's my bottom line: I like both the hand bump and the handshake, but each gesture communicates a slightly different intensity.

The traditional handshake goes back to medieval times when opponents used it to indicate they were friendly and unarmed. The handshake has been a part of business since the beginning of commerce. Anyone being advised on how to make a good impression in a job interview is counseled against the "limp celery" handshake. It must be firm but not a bone crusher, timed perfectly so it's not too long or too short, and certainly not look like a pumping oil derrick. That's a lot to consider when extending one's hand. Once satisfied you are not holding a concealed weapon, the handshake recipient must determine what is being communicated: eagerness, acceptance, distrust, disinterest, insecurity . . . the list goes on.

All those handshake precautions are not an issue with a fist bump. That merely involves two people tapping fists lightly and then moving on. There are advantages to that quick bump. If you look as if you are a walking case of bubonic plague, I'll do the bump and then flee in the opposite direction, satisfied we connected but only for a germless second. However, the fist bump can be simply and warmly interpreted as "I'm for you . . . Nice job . . . I enjoyed our time . . . Loved your speech . . . I'm here for you . . . Too bad you can't beat me in tennis . . . Better luck next time."

The fist bump is frequently used with athletes as they offer encouragement or congratulations to each other. When time is not an issue, they can shake hands and look into each other's eyes, and the communication registers at a deeper level.

Several years ago, those of us on The Porch at Women of Faith events established the tradition of each of us walking down the speaker row and shaking hands before going on the platform. It is a sweet time of comforting encouragement as we feel the grip of a hand we know is communicating, "I'll be praying that God blesses your words." (I also want added to their prayer that he'll unclutter my brain and supply my missing nouns.) That communication could occur with a fist bump, but sometimes I want a deeper encouragement that comes with a warm, whole hand.

There is interesting history about the hand as not only a communicator of encouragement but also of physical healing. The "laying on of hands" is an ancient custom that has been practiced for centuries—it was once known as "the king's touch." Ancient royalty touched their "subjects" in various healing rites, which was apparently thought to be effective; however, Queen Anne in 1712 could not seem to get the hang of it, so the healing rites slowly became royal history. But even though royalty stopped the healing rite, the belief lingered on into the twentieth century in the form of medallions bearing the royal image to which the power of the royal touch had hopefully been transferred.

We as Christians read in Matthew 8:1–3 of the practice of Jesus: "When He had come down from the mountain, great multitudes followed Him. And behold, a leper came and worshiped Him, saying, 'Lord, if You are willing, You can make me clean.' Then Jesus put out His hand and touched him, saying, 'I am willing; be cleansed.' Immediately his leprosy was cleansed" (NKJV). And then again, Mark describes Jesus: "Then they brought little children to Him, that He might touch them . . . and He took them up in His arms, laid His hands on them, and blessed them" (Mark 10:13, 16 NKJV).

What tender, sweet images these are of Jesus touching, healing, and affirming his dearly loved creation. Ancient royalty had not created their subjects, nor could they heal and comfort them as our Father God can.

Our desire for touch goes far beyond "That would be nice." Touch is mandatory for human health and even human existence. We literally do not thrive without it. You may remember the account from 1915 when a New York pediatrician, in a report on children's institutions in ten different U.S. cities, made the staggering discovery that in all but one institution, every infant under two years of age died. Why?

If a baby is to survive and to prosper, he or she must be handled, carried, caressed, cuddled, and cooed over. None of those precious babies were physically nurtured. There were too many babies and too few caregivers. We now use the phrase "failure to thrive" and fully understand what it means.

We were created to be touched from the moment we were born. One of the miracles of creation is skin. It is the oldest and the most sensitive of our organs, our first pathway for communication and most efficient protector. The skin has receptors that wordlessly communicate to a baby's brain whether there is love in his or her new environment. No touch, rough touch, infrequent touch, or angry touch—all are communicated through the newborn's skin. There is an interpretation of touch long before an interpretation of words.

I have a dear friend, Jan Davidson, who volunteers each Monday morning to hold, caress, and rock babies in the nursery at Children's Medical Center in Dallas. These are babies with severe physical challenges: some are anticipating surgery and others are recovering from surgery. Jan told me that last Monday a nurse gently replaced the baby Jan was rocking with another baby. The nurse whispered, "He does not have long . . . rock him into eternity." I know Jan's touch was a tender foretaste of what that baby soon experienced in the arms of his Creator.

Knowing how crucial touch is to the human soul, I appreciate the fist bump and the handshake; each is a connection to the core of my person.

But my favorite gesture of love and support is a hug. A hug gathers me up from head to toe into a place of full-bodied security. For that moment, when I am fully encompassed by arms I have no reason to mistrust, by a body without erotic intent, and by a spirit of gentle empathy, I experience rest.

A hug says simply, "I want to fully embrace all that you are and all that you feel. I want to communicate to you that for this moment nothing and no one has my focus except you."

A hug for a child can feel like life and death. Mother's arms soothe and quiet the little soul until all tears are wiped away and the rigors of the world can once again be faced with renewed confidence.

A hug provides not only shelter, comfort, and focus; it can also be an exuberant expression of "I'm so glad to see you, I just have to wrap you up and jump up and down!" (For some of us, those kinds of hugs require that we wear a little sign around our necks saying, "Easy does it—my bones make cracking sounds.")

I cannot imagine leaving this earth and upon my entry through the portals of heaven, God's greeting to me is a fist bump or a handshake. Absolutely not! I envision I will receive the physically exuberant response the prodigal son received when he returned home. That father did not even wait for the son to get within hug-distance. Instead, the father ran to him and gathered him up into a full-body hug of jubilant love. For that wonderful moment in time, the son knew he had been forgiven and welcomed home.

If you're needing a reminder of the Father's loving touch, munch on these words from Isaiah 40:10–11 (NKJV):

Behold, the Lord GOD shall come with a strong hand,
And His arm shall rule for Him:
Behold, His reward is with Him,
And His work before Him.
He will feed His flock like a shepherd;
He will gather the lambs with His arm,
And carry them in His bosom,
And gently lead those who are with young.

2

Our Shepherd

Sheila Walsh

> *Comfort, comfort my people, says your God . . . See, the Sovereign LORD comes with power, and his arm rules for him. See, his reward is with him, and his recompense accompanies him. He tends his flock like a shepherd: He gathers the lambs in his arms and carries them close to his heart; he gently leads those that have young.*
>
> —Isaiah 40:1, 10–11 NIV

grew up in farm country on the west coast of Scotland, and spring was always my favorite season. Spring said good-bye to long, dark winters and barren trees, and it promised extended sunlight and flowers pressing their way through the hard soil. Winter is a cold, gloomy season in Scotland. When I would wake up for school, it was dark; by the time I came home, it was dark again. We had a treasured flower garden underneath the living room window right outside the back door, and all winter long it was empty. Some days I would bundle up in a warm coat, scarf, and hat and sit at the edge of the flower bed and stare at the unforgiving soil. It was frozen over and lifeless; I couldn't imagine that anything was alive in there. I knew that we had planted crocuses, snowdrops, and bluebells. But the winter could be so unforgiving, and I would wonder if this was the one year that they just couldn't survive. Every morning I would take a flashlight outside before heading off for the school bus and check to see if there was even a sign of life. I still remember the pure joy I felt when I could see just the tiniest shoot begin to do the impossible and fight its way into the light. Even as a child, that sight spoke to me of hope and new beginnings. But my very favorite thing of all that spring promised was a fresh troop of spring lambs.

There is nothing quite as exuberant as newly born spring lambs. They jump and dance on wobbly legs as if they can hear a music that is hidden from the rest of the world. They make funny little bleating noises like a boy growing into manhood whose voice is unpredictable and surprising even to him. We get more than our fair share of rain on the west coast, but that also means our fields of grass are a vibrant green and the lambs look freshly scrubbed every morning. We are known for our sheep in that part of the country, and it was never more than a short bike ride to watch another field of jumping wonder.

One of the scenes that is still most vivid in my mind is watching the shepherd and his sheepdog rally the flock together and get them into their holding pen. The shepherd would come behind the flock and his well-trained dog responded to every short whistle and command. The sheep never looked ready to be corralled and did very little to help. Even though this ritual had taken place hundreds of times, they still looked surprised, but the sheepdog was as ready and prepared as a Navy Seal. Within no time at all, every sheep and every lamb was safely tucked inside the pen, and the dog took his place by the shepherd's feet once more.

So this is the picture that I have always carried in my mind when I read that Jesus tends his flock like a shepherd. I have imagined him gently coaxing me into the right place with a little prodding to the right or to the left when I'm not as cooperative as I might be. I have discovered, though, that this is not the picture that would come to the mind of anyone in Israel who thinks of the relationship between sheep and shepherd. In Palestine, you will never see a shepherd coming behind his sheep; he always goes ahead. He goes ahead to check that the path is safe and there are no wild animals that might attack the flock. When he crosses a stream and the sheep seem reluctant to follow, he picks up the youngest lamb of the flock and carries it on his shoulders, and the rest then follow. It is a very tender, relational picture. In Scotland, sheep and lambs are bred to be slaughtered for their meat but not so in Israel. In Israel, they are kept for their wool, so the shepherd has them for many years and often knows them by name. World-renowned travel writer H. V. Morton tells a story of observing two shepherds with their flocks one night on a Bethlehem hillside. The shepherds led the flocks into a limestone cave for the night, and Morton wondered how they would separate the sheep in the morning, as they had no obvious markings. At first light, one of the shepherds stood on a rock outside the cave and delivered a very peculiar whistle. At the sound, every one of his sheep came out and followed him, and the other sheep remained in the cave. They recognized the sound; they knew his voice.

Once I read that fact, I took another look at what John tells us in his Gospel about the Good Shepherd and discovered that the picture had been there all along:

> The man who enters by the gate is the shepherd of his sheep. The watchman opens the gate for him, and the sheep listen to his voice. He calls his own sheep by name and leads them out. When he has brought out all his own, he goes on ahead of them, and his sheep follow him because they know his voice. (John 10:2–4 NIV)

I find that picture deeply comforting. We have a shepherd who goes ahead of us to prepare the way. He looks for danger, for those who might harm us, and leads us on the path that he has chosen. We don't serve a Savior who tries to squeeze us into tight places or forces us to go afraid out into the unknown. No, he goes ahead of us, and we follow him because we know his voice. I have a little prayer that I pray every morning when I first wake up: "Father, I don't know where you are going today, but wherever you are going, I'm coming with you!"

I have discovered that the safest place to be is where Jesus is. It might not always look like the safest, but if that is where Jesus is, that is where I want to be. As you look at your life today, let me ask you a few questions.

What comes to your mind when you think of a shepherd?

What do you believe is the role of the sheep?

Have you ever known of a sheep worrying about what tomorrow might bring?

Will you trust the One who loves you and leads you?

One day, as we follow our Shepherd, we will find that the pasture has led us all the way home.

> *The King of love my Shepherd is,*
> *Whose goodness faileth never,*
> *I nothing lack if I am His*
> *And He is mine forever.*
> *Where streams of living water flow*
> *My ransomed soul He leadeth,*

And where the verdant pastures grow,
With food celestial feedeth.
And so through all the length of days
Thy goodness faileth never;
Good Shepherd, may I sing Thy praise
Within Thy house forever.
—"The King of Love My Shepherd Is"
Henry Williams Baker, 1868

3

Barbara's Legacy

....

Mary Graham

$\mathcal{J}$n the spring of 1996, I had my first encounter with Barbara Johnson. Earlier that year, I had met her briefly when I visited my first Women of Faith event, as it was just getting started. Barbara had written many books by then, including several best sellers like *Where Does a Mother Go to Resign?* and *I'm So Glad You Told Me What I Didn't Want to Know* and *Mama, Get the Hammer, There's a Fly on Papa's Head*. I hadn't read the books, but I had certainly heard a lot about Barbara.

Most of what I'd heard was about the tragic circumstances of her life. Two of her sons had been killed and a third one left home, walking out of a relationship with his parents to pursue a gay lifestyle. I'd heard she was at the time the best-selling female Christian author . . . *ever*. I'd heard she was funny, and I'd been warned she was really, really feisty.

What no one told me was that beneath all that incredible strength that enabled her to survive was a heart that was wide-open to others and tender to anyone who needed anything. And I certainly hadn't anticipated that she (for whatever reason I'll never understand) would love me like a daughter. No one has ever been more generous, caring, or truly committed to me. Through very strange circumstances that no one but God himself could have engineered, I became "unofficially" (at first) a part of the organization called Women of Faith, and Barbara, the feisty one, became my biggest cheerleader.

It didn't start out that way. My first "official" meeting with the team was in April of 1996. I'd flown to California from Florida to talk with the speakers about Women of Faith. The founder of the organization, Steve Arterburn, had invited me to help with the programming of the event. Marilyn Meberg and Luci Swindoll were longtime friends of mine, but Patsy Clairmont and Barbara were new to me. I'd only heard them speak at Women of Faith a time or two. This brand-new event was just getting started.

For that first meeting, just before Easter, I decided to create little baskets for the four women. (Having no children of my own, I've always treated adult friends like children during all the holidays.) Luci, Patsy, and Marilyn were as gleeful as five-year-olds when they saw those baskets. Barbara, however, in her first words to me said, "I can't have this! I'm a diabetic." (I guess she hadn't noticed there were a lot of little treasures in the basket that were *not* candy.) I took it, set it aside, and dived into the meeting.

Marilyn and Luci were very supportive of me, and Patsy was kind, adorable, and very engaged throughout the meeting. (And they were as giddy as children about their baskets!) As far as I could tell, Barbara was planning to shoot me if I'd just shut up.

But, I could not have been more mistaken about Barbara. She became my devoted friend, my trusted comrade, and my most loyal defender. And it had absolutely nothing to do with me. There were thousands, and I might not be exaggerating when I say she had tens of thousands, of people for whom she'd literally lay down her life. In fact, I might have been one of a million.

Soon we were all on the road together all the time, in and out of airports, taxicabs, hotels, and arenas. We were doing photo shoots and music videos (which Barbara said were "stupid" from the beginning, but she was cooperative). Through it all, we became friends and a wonderfully fun and enjoyable team. We bonded in our hearts and minds with this amazing vision that we could actually bring women together for encouragement, insight about God and his ways, great music, hearty laughter, and a few tears. Women all over the country were saying, "This changed my life," and that kept us going. Behind the scenes, I was amazed at what I saw and heard. I was astounded by how much I loved the speaker team, the audience, and especially what I sensed God was doing as we kept getting more and more bonded as a team and increasingly encouraged by everything we saw. We were working hard but becoming more energized every day. As diverse as we all were, we knew God was bonding us as a team and in friendships that would last a lifetime.

But nobody was like Barbara Johnson. People loved her on the platform although she never played by our "rules." She just did what made sense to her, and for some reason, it worked. She always had the longest lines at her book table, probably because she talked with everyone personally. I gave up trying to get her to "behave" because it didn't matter. She was feisty, formidable at times, completely predictable, yet absolutely unpredictable. She was an original—a person of unique design. And I loved her dearly, just like the world did.

Barbara understood the pain of life, and it drove her to love, give, support, encourage, and defend others.

I remember a time many years ago in Charlotte, North Carolina, at Women of Faith. A woman who'd been seriously abused was hiding in a bar on Friday night and saw Barbara interviewed on a local TV show. The woman somehow was able to get from that downtown bar to the arena on Saturday by noon. She spoke to some attendees who were having lunch on the lawn and asked, "Can I talk with Barbara Johnson?" She had no idea she was one of twenty thousand attending that day who wanted to talk with her. The women saw her need and contacted a Women of Faith staff member, who contacted me. I asked Barbara, knowing that her response would be, "Bring her down here."

When the staff brought her to Barbara, the woman was obviously in physical as well as spiritual need. She had spent the night hiding from a man who was trying to kill her. Barbara took her to the locker room (a side advantage of meeting in arenas, I suppose) and helped her shower. She sent us all scurrying to find clean clothes, which we did. Barbara was like Jesus to her. The rest of us were in tears. I heard Barbara ask, "Do you know anyone in the world who loves you?" The woman said she had a grandmother in Illinois who did. Barbara said, "If you go there, will you be safe?" When the woman said she would, Barbara put cash in the woman's pocket and told our staff to go with her to the train station to be sure she got a ticket to the only person on the earth the woman knew loved her.

Then we all went back in the arena and went on with the event as if we had not just witnessed a miracle. Sooner or later, I suppose, we came to expect that from Barbara. She was like Jesus. She wouldn't give you a nickel if you were pious, but if you were in need, she embraced you. If you were comfortable, she might not even acknowledge you. But if you were distressed, finding her would be all the comfort you'd ever need. Few people really saw this side of Barbara. Fewer still know that, before she died, she got a commitment from me to provide free tickets every weekend for people who could not afford the Women of Faith event. In every event, there is a "Barbara Johnson Legacy" section. And we continue to get mail from those women who've been encouraged by her gift. Her legacy lives on. Interestingly, when she comforted others, we were comforted.

Barbara Johnson was a crusty old soul at times. She had a mind of her own; she was incorrigible and hopelessly nonconforming. But if you had needs and she knew it, she'd take care of you in a heartbeat. If she loved you, you were set for life.

And, in the most amazing way, she left all of us this legacy from 2 Thessalonians 2:16–17: "Now may our Lord Jesus Christ Himself and God our Father, who has loved us and given us eternal comfort and good hope by grace, comfort and strengthen your hearts in every good work and word" (NASB).

4

Andrew's Story

....

Mandisa

Probably like most public figures in America, I enjoy meeting and corresponding with the people who support what I do. At the conclusion of almost all of my shows, I sit at a tall table with a bottle of water and a black Sharpie and greet hundreds of smiling faces with pictures, books, T-shirts, and CDs in hand. On rare occasions, I am humbled by a teenage girl so amazed that she is posing next to me for a picture that she shakes in my arms and leaves in a puddle of tears. Typically her mom sweeps her away and whispers, "She's your biggest fan."

I love meeting my "biggest fans." As a former contestant on *American Idol*, I know all too well the power of fans. It is fans who voted for me, pray for me, purchase my albums, and come to my concerts. The least I can do in return is sign a few items and say, "Cheese."

Of course, social networking has brought being a

public figure to a whole new level. The invention of MySpace, Facebook, and Twitter has narrowed the gap between fan and celebrity. My "tweeps" (Twitter friends) know all about me: when I exercise, what I eat, and what kind of man I'd like to marry (BIG, black, born-again believer with a bald head and a goatee . . . in case you were wondering). With the number of social networking sites, it's no wonder that my manager hired a full-time staff person to manage most of mine. Still, even with the rigors of concerts, interviews, writing, and recording, I like to stay connected as much as I can, so every so often I hop onto one of my sites and catch up on a few messages.

One such day happened in April 2008. I logged onto MySpace and saw dozens of messages in my in-box (apparently my Internet guru had been a little busy). I hunkered down and began chipping away at what felt to me like a massive amount of work. The first twenty or so required only quick responses: "Where did you get that blouse you wore on *Extra*?" "When is your next album coming out?" "Are you coming to Iowa anytime soon?" I breezed through them in less than thirty minutes. Then I saw the message that would leave an indelible mark on my heart. It was from a lady who introduced herself as Cheryl. She wrote that her best friend, Rebecca, was my biggest fan. Rebecca had followed me since my time on *American Idol*. I was the only person she'd ever voted for, and she had boycotted the show after my elimination. She read my book,

Idoleyes and knew every word to every song on my debut album, *True Beauty*. Then Cheryl revealed that Rebecca and her husband, Billy, were pregnant with their first child and Cheryl was throwing them a baby shower in a few weeks. The reason for her letter was to ask if I would be willing to write a short message Cheryl could read at the shower.

I was so touched by Cheryl's love for Rebecca that I quickly hit "Respond" and began typing away. In less than fifteen minutes I had composed a one-page letter for Cheryl to surprise Rebecca with at her shower. In it I shared that my best friend was also pregnant with her first child. I quoted Psalm 139 and shared that God was knitting that precious little baby in her womb. I thanked her for her support and hoped that one day I would be able to meet her in person. I had no idea that day would come less than a month later.

My band and I had a concert at Whitesburg Baptist Church in Huntsville, Alabama—Rebecca's hometown! Of course I noticed the very pregnant woman sitting in the front row mouthing every word to each of my fifteen songs, but I didn't find out it was Rebecca until my signing after the concert. She was the second person in line (one teenage girl apparently beat her to the chase). Before she even opened her mouth, I could sense her excitement. She had a smile that radiated through the entire room. Her brown, bob-cut, shoulder-length hair matched her brown eyes glowing with anticipation.

As the teenage girl moved to my right, Rebecca lunged forward. With one breath and in no less than two hundred high-pitched words, she explained that she was the Rebecca I had written a baby shower blessing to. In an instant, my excitement matched hers. We squealed, hugged, and tried to take in the moment. She was delighted to be meeting me, while I was blown away at God's providence. After I did my best to memorize her face, I turned my attention to her bulging belly. She shared that she was due in just nine days and that the name she and her husband had chosen was Andrew.

I gently laid my hand on her stomach and prayed for sleeping Andrew. Once again with Psalm 139 as my guide, I prayed that God would carefully create Andrew's inmost being to be fearfully and wonderfully made. I ended by proclaiming that all the days ordained for Andrew would be written in his Creator's book before one of them came to be. Finally, growing aware of the patiently waiting line of people behind us, Rebecca and I said our good-byes, and she cheerfully waddled away.

Seven days later, I received this urgent message from her friend Cheryl: "Rebecca and her husband really need your prayers right now. Rebecca went into labor this morning, and when they got to the hospital, the baby had no heartbeat. We have no explanation for what happened. Rebecca will deliver hopefully by tonight, and we will have a funeral for little Andrew next week."

I stared at my computer screen for what felt like a paralyzing hour. Surely this was some sort of mistake. I had just seen Rebecca seven days ago. She was fine. Happy. Healthy. I had just prayed for Andrew. Remember, God? All the days being ordained for Andrew? As I tried to reason it out, I grew angry. I yelled at God! "How could you let this happen? If you were going to take Andrew, couldn't you have done it sooner? What were you thinking?" Then in the middle of my furious rampage, the song I had sung on my album *True Beauty* came to mind. The melody of "God Speaking" began swirling around in my head: "His ways are higher. His ways are better."

As my bitterness subsided, the Holy Spirit focused my mind on things above. In that moment, I understood that God was weeping along with Rebecca and Billy, that God understood all too well how it feels to lose one's only Son. I cried. Then I prayed. Then I cried some more.

I reread Cheryl's message and only then noticed she had ended her letter by asking me, if I felt led, to write another message to Rebecca. The two-page letter poured out of me as quickly as the tears. In it, I explained that I believe wholeheartedly in the power of Scripture. I wrote a list of ten things I was praying for her, along with the Scripture references. Number 1 was for God's comfort (Psalm 34:18). Number 10 was for God to eventually use her to minister to others who have gone through a similar tragedy (2 Corinthians 1:3–7).

Fast-forward two years. Rebecca and I have become great friends. While Andrew will always be her first child, her daughter, Katie Lane, was born in September 2009. On my second album, *Freedom*, I memorialized her story in a song titled "You Wouldn't Cry (Andrew's Song)." Since then, I have shared her story on television, on video, and on countless stages all across the country.

Afterward, in my signings, I am always overwhelmed by the number of women who share how much they identify with Rebecca's story. They explain that "Andrew's Song" has been a source of encouragement and hope for them. I love telling Rebecca about the stories I hear and the people I meet whom she has had a tremendous impact on. And it never ceases to amaze me when she in turn tells me of someone she has met, shared her testimony with, and ended up ministering to. Recently, she has even been asked to lead a group at her church for women who have faced the death of a child.

Rebecca, Billy, and Andrew have taught me that, often, great comfort is bred from great heartache. For it is through our pain that we grow in wisdom and compassion. We serve a God who is well acquainted with our sufferings. Only God can comfort us in our pain and then allow us to transfer that comfort to others.

All praise to God, the Father of our Lord Jesus Christ. God is our merciful Father and the source of all comfort. He comforts us in all our troubles so that we can comfort others. When they are troubled, we will be able to give them the same comfort God has given us. For the more we suffer for Christ, the more God will shower us with his comfort through Christ. Even when we are weighed down with troubles, it is for your comfort and salvation! For when we ourselves are comforted, we will certainly comfort you. Then you can patiently endure the same things we suffer. We are confident that as you share in our sufferings, you will also share in the comfort God gives us. (2 Corinthians 1:3–7 NLT)

5

Wounded Healers

. . . .

Lisa Harper

As a middle-aged, single woman, sometimes I find holiday commercials depicting close-knit families in matching sweaters gathered around a dinner table decorated with sweet potato casserole, green beans, hot cross buns, and a bronzed turkey a tad depressing. Especially when I'm watching them while I'm sitting on the couch in sweatpants with a Lean Cuisine in my lap. Mind you, my life has never looked like a Norman Rockwell painting, but the American ideal of a husband, wife, and two happy children model that's peddled everywhere at Thanksgiving and Christmastime pokes the bruises in my heart.

Adding insult to injury, my disappointment culminated in a fender bender this past Christmas Eve. There I was, dutifully trying to focus on cheerful things—to *set my mind on things above*—as I packed the car to drive to Alabama to be with my sister and her family. Assuming some rock music would put a kick in my step, I dialed my iPod to the Black Eyed Peas' song, "Boom Boom Pow." I thought replacing Amy Grant with a little Fergie would be harmless. What I didn't bargain for was how loud the bass was in my new integrated car stereo system. It wasn't until I wondered, *Why in the world is the garage door taking so long to go up?* for the second time that I realized it was caught on the back of my car!

Trust me on this, a mangled garage door and giant dent in the car you've only had for a few months does not prompt visions of sugarplums dancing in your head.

During seasons when the reality of my life doesn't remotely resemble the one in my dreams, I pine for a different kind of Messiah. One who will make all my disappointments disappear. One who will answer my prayer for a husband and children. One who will make my closest friends interested listeners and conscientious encouragers—and chubbier than I am. Sometimes I just wish Jesus would make life easier.

Of course, a Messiah who only served to grant our wishes would be akin to an overly indulgent mother who let her child eat all the candy he wanted, let him stay up as late as he liked, and never encouraged him to accept responsibility or to obey authority. Pretty soon, the result is a middle-aged man with no job, no friends, and no respect for her, who is still living in his boyhood bedroom and demanding Twinkies for lunch. If Jesus were like the overindulgent mother, we'd never grow up. We'd never learn to love others well or have hope beyond our current circumstances. We'd have no real peace or lasting joy.

Jesus didn't die to make us happy. He's not some cartoon character flitting around in a sparkly outfit and waving a magic wand. He's the sovereign Son of the Most High God. And he sacrificed his life because that was the only way to reconcile sinners like us with that very same God. Jesus died so we could get to know our heavenly Father. He suffered all the way to death on a cross so that we could be saved. As a matter of fact, the author of Hebrews says suffering is actually what prepared him for Golgotha: "Even though Jesus was the Son of God, he learned obedience by what he suffered" (Hebrews 5:8 NCV).

Communing with Jesus on a deep level without experiencing some wounds of our own is about as realistic as being a champion swimmer who never gets wet. Frankly, communing with *anybody* on a deep level is impossible for Pollyanna types because God has plopped us in a world filled with heartache. Seemingly happy couples go through mean-spirited divorces that divide their possessions and rip their kids right down the middle. Innocents are brutalized in the sex slave trade. Millions die every year because they have no access to clean water. The AIDS epidemic still rages. Cherub-faced babies are born with incurable cancer and heart defects. The neighbors next door lose their house to foreclosure. Graduating seniors can't get jobs.

Grandparents get Alzheimer's. We can't expect to make a difference in that kind of world—with those kinds of broken people—unless we can empathize with their pain and disappointment.

Now before you toss this devotional to the floor and start gobbling Ben and Jerry's out of despair, let me remind you of two huge knots we can hang on to when we get to the end of our proverbial rope. The first one is God's promise to be close to the brokenhearted: "The LORD is close to the brokenhearted, and he saves those whose spirits have been crushed" (Psalm 34:18 NCV).

Our Creator is not a fair-weather friend. He will not abandon us in our anguish. It doesn't matter if you're one of those ugly criers whose face gets all red and blotchy. It doesn't matter if your nose and mascara run. It doesn't matter if you become a big, whiny "woe is me" baby. God still won't walk away. He won't roll his eyes at your drama or throw his hands up in exasperation. He holds us the entire time our shoulders are heaving. And much like a new mom keeps track of every peep her infant makes, so our heavenly Father counts each and every tear that rolls down his children's cheeks: "You have kept count of my tossings; put my tears in your bottle" (Psalm 56:8a ESV).

The second knot is the beauty that comes with the buffeting. Remember the old Skin Horse in Margery Williams' classic children's book, *The Velveteen Rabbit*? His fur had been worn off in places, and most of the hairs in

his tail had been pulled out by kids to make necklaces—
in other words, life had left him a bit worn around the
edges—but that's what made him *real*:

> "What is REAL?" asked the Rabbit one day, when they
> were lying side by side near the nursery fender, before
> Nana came to tidy the room. "Does it mean having
> things that buzz inside you and a stick-out handle?"
>
> "Real isn't how you are made," said the Skin
> Horse. "It's a thing that happens to you. When a child
> loves you for a long, long time, not just to play with,
> but REALLY loves you, then you become Real."
>
> "Does it hurt?" asked the Rabbit.
>
> "Sometimes," said the Skin Horse, for he was
> always truthful. "When you are Real you don't mind
> being hurt."
>
> "Does it happen all at once, like being wound up,"
> he asked, "or bit by bit?"
>
> "It doesn't happen all at once," said the Skin
> Horse. "You become. It takes a long time. That's why
> it doesn't happen often to people who break easily, or
> have sharp edges, or who have to be carefully kept.
> Generally, by the time you are Real, most of your hair
> has been loved off, and your eyes drop out and you get
> loose in your joints and very shabby. But these things
> don't matter at all, because once you are Real you can't
> be ugly, except to people who don't understand."

I wonder if Margery Williams was inspired by Paul's second letter to Christians living in Corinth because that was essentially the heart of his message too: "All praise to God, the Father of our Lord Jesus Christ. God is our merciful Father and the source of all comfort. He comforts us in all our troubles so that we can comfort others. When they are troubled, we will be able to give them the same comfort God has given us" (2 Corinthians 1:3–4 NLT).

Just as the Skin Horse's bald spots prove he'd been loved, the scars on our hearts authenticate our ability to help others who are in pain. The bumps in our journey enable us to help others navigate rough spots. We can soothe those around us who are suffering because we've been there. We can credibly testify that during our darkest days, when we didn't feel like we had the strength to take one more step, God carried us. Frankly, I think true compassion has to be forged in the kiln of ache. Henri Nouwen said it well in *The Wounded Healer*: "The great illusion of leadership is to think that man can be led out of the desert by someone who has never been there" (New York: Doubleday, 1972).

So the next time you find yourself limping through a valley of life or longing to hurl frozen food at your television during the holidays, hang tight to God's immediate mercy and comfort as well as to the fact that he will ultimately use your experience as medicine for another sick sojourner.

6

A Place Called Home

. . . .

Patsy Clairmont

The ache for home lives in all of us.
—Maya Angelou

Recently I walked my feet into nubbins as I hiked around town on a home tour. Up and down streets, up and down hallways, and up and down stairwells. It was a wonderfully exhausting stint. I love looking at homes: old homes, new homes, rambling homes, and cottages. Especially cottages with gardens. And I love historical homes, something significantly older than me that's still standing. (It comforts me.) When I tour, I like to see different architectural designs and individuals' decorating sensibilities and discover creative innovations I might take home and apply.

My home interest has probably grown out of my mom's addiction. My mother was a house addict, and now I'm chugging her "drug" of choice. And when I say drug, I mean it because, throughout my childhood, I was drug from one home to another with my family's frequent moves.

As a kid, I was more than a reluctant mover, I left skid marks between homes from dragging my attitude. I actually liked every residence we lived in, but never at first. I hated bare walls, windows, and floors. And while I didn't have trouble making new friends, I was always sad leaving old playmates.

Yet before long, I'd meet children who would become my pals, and Mom would soon coax every room into a warm environment full of simple beauties and inviting corners. I remember her standing for hours ironing curtains, doilies, and tablecloths, and then she'd go into action and work her magic. What had looked barren to my young eyes became lush with her loving touches. She knew how to take a little bit and fluff it into a wholesome surrounding.

I was surprised when I married my husband, Les, that he, like my mom, liked to change residences . . . frequently. We've been married forty-eight years, so I've packed a lot of boxes and faced many shadeless windows and naked floors. We have lived in apartments, farm houses, mobile homes, bungalows, cottages, and currently a newer home. So I guess it's a good thing my mom prepared me for disruption via change. The two of them, Les and Mom, have helped to keep me from my tendency of holding on too tight. Sorta.

Somewhere during the hopscotching of homes, I caught the house bug, and I've been hoofing tours, watching HGTV, and overdosing on home magazines ever since. At least once a month, my hubby suggests we buy a motor home and take our abode everywhere we go. My answer is consistent because my soul needs the anchor of a single location: I don't want my only home to be on wheels, although I know there are those who love it. I think I've moved too often for that much of a vagabond lifestyle.

I've wondered about Old Testament Sarah. How did she adjust to her nomadic moves? She didn't wheel-it, but she did walk-it . . . and she tented-it. Tent? Eek! Honestly, dealing with the desert dust puts my allergies on high alert. Not to mention if hubby would be always tracking in camel droppings. Think about it . . . that's no small matter.

Poor Sarah had to walk up and down deserts, up and down mountains, through oases—just to get to the grocery store for milk and honey. Hers was not a delivery-service neighborhood.

Yes, I have to believe pulling up stakes (literally) for Sarah was no Grand Canyon spree. And I bet that, years later, Sarah would have made an empathetic mentor for Old Testament Ruth had she crossed her grief-stricken path. You see, after tragedy struck Ruth's home, she chose to uproot herself from the safety of all she'd ever known to go to a place she'd never been, so, like Sarah, she was on a new house hunt. Only Ruth was a widow who had just left the fresh graveside of her husband, and she would travel with her bitter mother-in-law to a place where Ruth most likely would be met with judgment and prejudicial treatment. I'm pretty sure Ruth would tell us it's not always easy moving into a new neighborhood and finding your place among reluctant strangers whose ways are unknown to you. It's as though you waltz in and they are all doing the jitterbug. It takes time to learn new rhythms.

As a speaker and writer, I find myself weekly setting up my "tent" among strangers in hotels across the nation. Each hotel is different in some respects and, unfortunately, similar in others. After hotel hopping for some twenty-five-plus years, I can reiterate the time-worn truth with passion, "There's no place like home." I love being on tour, but I must say, when I drive into my neighborhood and spot my abode, tension begins to drain out of my body.

My hubby and I had occasion at one juncture of our lives to "live" in a hotel for almost four months. Yes, months. May I just say that's too long . . . even if they do make your bed and leave you a bar of soap. I can't imagine how long Sarah had to stay in the swirling desert, changing tents sometimes daily. Or how long Ruth carried the broken heart of her mother-in-law down a long, dusty road before she arrived in the fields of Boaz. But

I guarantee you that as they trudged ahead, their hearts longed for home . . . where they were known, loved, and where they knew which way to turn to get to Target.

Oh, did I mention we're moving again? This one is a biggie because it will take us out of our home state of Michigan, which is where we've tended to roam for more than sixty years, to the state of Tennessee, y'all. We've chosen a historical "tent" this time, which should be hysterical, as well as redundant. It's a lovely home in a place we feel received and even celebrated. How inviting.

Sometimes I wonder if my interest in houses is really spurred on not by my mom's hobby, but by a longing for "home." That state where the heart never stops rejoicing and where one settles into an eternal abode. The book of Ecclesiastes tells us eternity has been set in our hearts. And in Hebrews 13:14, we read, "For here we have no continuing city, but we seek the one to come" (NKJV).

7

My Brilliant Babe

. . . .

Luci Swindoll

I have a feeling you've probably heard of my brother, Chuck Swindoll. In my opinion, Chuck is the finest Bible teacher in America today. He's bright, knowledgeable, practical, creative, warm, relevant, and extremely funny—a rare combination of superlative gifts in all categories, blended together in a vessel God has chosen to use mightily. *Of course you'd say that, Luci,* you're thinking to yourself. *He's your brother.* There is some truth to that, I admit. I am biased. We're not only bound together in family unity but in spiritual unity as well.

Chuck is the younger of my two brothers, and when we were children, Mother would say to me, "Go see about the baby," so I would toddle into where he was lying or playing, check on things, and report back to Mother. At that early point in time, I began calling Chuck "Baby" or "Babe," and for seventy-five years, that's been his name with me: Babe. He's my *Babe*. I'm the only one in the entire family who calls him that.

Among the numerous questions asked of me as I travel and speak for Women of Faith is, "How does it feel to be Chuck Swindoll's sister?" While I find that a somewhat odd question, I know why people ask it. I'd probably ask it myself were I *not* his sister. But I can answer it immediately and without contemplation: it feels great! I love Babe. Deeply. I'm inordinately proud of his many accomplishments: a fine musician, a magna cum laude graduate from Dallas Theological Seminary (and thirty-two years later, its president), a prolific author of books too numerous to count, president of Insight for Living (a worldwide, daily radio ministry that's been going strong for thirty-one years), an incomparable speaker, pastor, leader, and one who holds four honorary doctorates. So, yeah! I think he's incredible. But my love for him is based on so much more than his academic achievements.

One of my favorite attributes that Babe had growing up was his learning and quoting poetry. He loved poetry (and still does). He memorized numerous poems, planting them firmly in his mind . . . never to be forgotten. And now when I hear him speak Sunday after Sunday, a poem he learned as a child will often sprout up like a full-grown tree, giving wonderful beauty and color to his sermon. I so admire that. It often moves me to tears and takes my mind back to our earliest childhood when we'd wrangle over who got to keep the little *Poems Every Child Should Know* in his or her bedroom that night. Somehow the remembrance of that gives me comfort and puts a smile on my face.

With all the talent Babe has, my favorite ability he has is his skill with words. While serving in the Marine Corps, he began considering the possibility of entering the ministry. For a period of time, he was stationed on the island of Okinawa and wrote all of us letters from there. I still have every one he sent me—each is a precious treasure. Just look at a portion of this one, written to me on May 4, 1958. He was responding to the fact that I had lost my job in a small company in Houston.

Dear "Sweets,"

Upon receiving Dad's last letter, I read of your position being terminated at the Exploration Company. Sis, dear, God has something greater for you. I have never seen it fail—God always puts us in the roughest situations at the strangest times. He delights in moving believers into new situations without even cluing us in on it. Whenever we become an effective witness by means of growth in the Word . . . God begins immediately putting us to the real test—that long, hard climb toward maturity. Remember, dear one, God continues to provide, even among the tests He places us under. You are now well on your way—suffering!

> *May I assure you of the prayers of your loving brother, who is too far away to be with you and visit you during these times of waiting and trusting, but knows very well the full impact of believing prayers.*

Oh, how that letter gave me comfort. Even though it was written years ago, I remember that feeling of comfort it conveyed as if it were yesterday. For him to take the time to write it meant the world to me . . . not to mention the love and tenderness in his words.

On Sundays, when Babe's in the pulpit, I often think of that passage in 2 Corinthians 1:3–4 in *The Message*: "All praise to the God and Father of our Master, Jesus the Messiah! Father of all mercy! God of all healing counsel! He comes alongside us when we go through hard times; and before you know it, he brings us alongside someone else who is going through hard times so that we can be there for that person just as God was there for us." There's so much comfort in all of that, and it's the message of encouragement we hear every Sunday from Babe.

What is it in Babe that makes him who he is? Of course, it's a combination of many gifts mixed with God's grace. But I also believe it's the fervent prayers of our mother. There wasn't a day in her life she didn't pray for her three children. Not one day. Surely, the Lord used those prayers to guide and direct each one of us. Mother had Scripture verses taped to the wall in front of the sink where she washed dishes, and one day Babe was running through the kitchen to go play football. He stopped for a minute and saw the verse she was learning that day, Proverbs 18:16: "A man's gift makes room for him and brings him before great men" (NASB). Babe asked why she was learning that particular verse. "I'm claiming it for all three of you children," she said. I feel sure her steady, consistent prayers are, in great part, what put Babe where he is today. She believed it, and God honored her prayers.

Here is something that can be a real comfort: there's no telling what can occur when mothers pray consistently for their kids. Scripture tells us that the constant prayers of a righteous person are very powerful. I believe Mother's faithfulness in praying had a profound effect on Babe, and I'm seeing the fruit of that today.

If you find yourself discouraged about your children—how they spend their time, who they hang with, where they go to have fun—pray for them. And if you're praying already, increase those prayers. I have no way of knowing what Mother asked the Lord regarding us, but I imagine it's the same thing you're asking for your children. Keep at it, and although it might take a long time, it will yield positive dividends.

I moved back to Texas seven years ago from having lived thirty years in Southern California primarily to be closer to the Women of Faith office and an airport for our weekend trips. But what did the Lord do in the meantime?

He moved Babe and his wife, Cynthia, about six blocks away from me. I didn't know that was going to happen when I moved to Frisco. And now, there they are . . . just down the street.

We're closer than we've ever been before. It's a gift of God's amazing grace! Sometimes, I think Philemon 1:7 was written just for Babe and me: "Your love has given me much joy and comfort, my brother, for your kindness has often refreshed the hearts of God's people" (NLT).

8

A Place Where We Can Rest

....

Lisa Whelchel

The original hope of the founder of World Vision was that hearts would be broken with the things that break the heart of God. In traveling to Rwanda with Luci, Marilyn, and Mary with World Vision in 2009, I felt that firsthand. My prayer upon starting this trip had been that my eyes would be opened to the degree that I could say, "I once was blind, but now I see." My prayer was answered.

From the very beginning of the trip, my eyes saw new things and some old things as if for the first time. The landscape of Rwanda was much more gorgeous than I anticipated. Beautiful mountains blanketed with lush greenery. The people have the brightest smiles I've ever encountered. I was mostly impressed by the awareness that each face had a unique story . . . filled with a heart-tugging mix of pain and joy. Our trip took us into the villages where we met so many of the people responsible for my new "sight."

One was a woman named Beatrice, whose story as it unfolds is truly inspiring. Her husband was in prison for participating in the genocide that received worldwide attention. While he was in prison, Beatrice had to fend for herself. She lived on land at the top of a hill that was beautiful for its landscape, but she and her daughter lived under a tarp—not even close to being sufficient shelter to protect them from the rainy seasons. When she heard that World Vision representatives were coming to the village and looking for "the poorest of the poor," she rushed to sign up. The community chose her daughter to be registered for a sponsorship.

Before long, the little girl received a World Vision sponsor. The support money bought Beatrice and her daughter food and shelter. World Vision determined that their most dire need was to have something more than a tarp, so a small cinder-block house was built. Beatrice was even hired to help build it. With the money she made from working on her house, she bought a single chicken. That chicken laid eggs, and Beatrice fed her family and sold the rest of the eggs. With the money she made from the eggs, she bought two pigs. The pigs reproduced—and she sold the little ones at market. With that money, she bought a cow. She used the milk to feed her family and the manure to fertilize the ground so she could plant a garden. Now she is organizing a co-op with other women in the village. She will help others as she has been helped. That was one of the most incredible stories I have heard.

We drove to a group of houses built by World Vision for families affected by and infected with HIV/AIDs. We met Klarissa, a gentle caregiver who was giving a sponge bath to a young woman and her baby boy. Klarissa was raped during the genocide by a man who purposely used AIDS as a weapon. She told her story, and it was almost too hard for us to hear. At the end of our visit, Luci beautifully ministered to us all by singing "Nobody Knows the Trouble I've Seen." Somewhere in the middle of the song, Klarissa transformed from a prematurely old woman, carrying the weight of the world, to a beautiful, young woman with a trace of joy expressed through a light-filled smile.

Another stop was to a World Vision school with almost 1,500 students, all either sponsored by World Vision or with a sibling sponsored. The students had prepared a little show for us, complete with lots of dancing. They even "volunteered" me to dance with them.

The thing that struck me the most about this school visit, other than the obviously wonderful work World Vision is doing by providing an education for so many children, is the commonalities these children have with our own children. Yes, they are on the other side of the world and living in little huts . . . but they are, first and foremost, children. Children just like the little ones I know in America. Giggly, mischievous, affectionate, curious, playful, and, in a word, childlike. And World Vision is helping them to be able to have a childhood—that's incredible!

Especially important to me on this trip was the opportunity I had to meet one of the children I sponsor. She is sweet, shy, four-year-old Josianne. I brought her a few small gifts, and she quietly received them. Then someone brought her a plate of food, and I began to feed her. She was so hungry, but not hungry enough to eat her peas. I guess children are the same everywhere!

After her tummy was full, she nestled into my chest, and I rocked her to sleep. I prayed quietly for her while she rested. I was struck in a fresh way with what a powerful privilege prayer is. I prayed that God would keep, bless, and heal her. I prayed for her family, her future spouse, and her future children, that their legacy would be different because of World Vision and these simple prayers, prayed in faith.

From now on, I know that I will include Josianne and our other sponsored children in my prayers for my own three children. This experience taught me to feel a much deeper level of responsibility for my sponsored children—not just financial support but prayer investment, as well.

The lessons I learned on this Rwanda trip will stay with me. I saw the results of one man's vision to help families throughout the world. I saw what can happen when people know they are needed and respond. I saw the value of prayer. And I truly saw the comfort of God.

As I held Josianne for more than an hour, and as she, trusting in me completely, slept peacefully, I knew that there is a part of all of us that longs to be fed in our emptiest places and then held until we nestle into a quiet rest and peace. In the times after my return from Rwanda when I have felt a longing in the pit of my soul, a fear in the presence of strangers, or worry about my future, I imagine that I am like little Josianne. I am snuggled up next to my heavenly Father, and he is responding to my ache and settling my uneasiness and comforting the hungry, scared little girl in me.

> *Safe in the arms of Jesus*
> *Safe on His gentle breast*
> *There by His love o'ershaded,*
> *Sweetly my soul doth rest.*
> —*"Safe in the Arms of Jesus"*
> Frances J. Crosby, 1868

Freedom

1

Plugging In

. . . .

Patsy Clairmont

*C*ords. And more cords. They are everywhere. At least in my world. And even though we are now considered a cordless generation, I spend a good deal of time looking for an outlet. It's so bad now I even carry cords in my purse. So for instance, when my phone signals me that it's low on energy, I whip that extension out and plug 'er in. If you are strictly a car, bus, or train person, you may not know that airports offer plug-in centers where you will find folks like me gathered around, eagerly waiting their turn to power up, so we can trot off to Kipsey and all points beyond.

At night, when it's time to go to sleep, you will find me wandering around my home, plugging things in. There's my iPad, which is my latest fun gadget, that must be charged overnight so I can access it at any given moment. Then there is my Kindle, in which I have a full library, that allows me to do research work anywhere. It, too, must be hooked up, but only every few days. My computer has to be recharged daily, so it's a must for an outlet, which I like to do before I drop into bed so it's fully ready to go with me to the local bakery or coffee shop in the morning (okay, noon). I often write at the bakery, but I try to get there early before all the selfish people beat me to the limited outlets that I know I'll need after a few hours of doughnuts and sweet iced tea. (Yep, I'm a health nut!) Then there's my ever-present iPhone, which, depending on how much I use it and for what, may require me to plug it in twice a day, which is why I don't like to leave home without its umbilical cord.

Talk about dependence. Talk about addiction. Talk about cords.

When you think about it, we start off with an umbilical cord, then grow into a "plug" (pacifier), and move on from there. Honestly, we (I) have enough electronics to justify owning our (my) own energy companies. My son is into green power sources and privately owned windmills to generate and store power. I wonder if those come in purse-size editions?

I love connection, whether it is calling a girlfriend on my cell, sending a text to a son, or e-mailing my boss for a raise (hint, hint). It comforts me to know they are a button push or voice command away. I know every generation has the same sense of how fortunate we are to live now instead of in the good ol' days. You may remember when you had to crank up your stationary phone, wait for an operator, and yell your request. Not to mention all the party-liners who often felt led to get involved in other people's conversations. *Party line* today has a whole new connotation, and we won't even go there.

In the days when phones didn't move, outlets were few and far between, and folks waited daily at their mailboxes for information about their loved ones. That was their connection, which meant it might be months before they heard from their children and friends, depending on how remote each one was.

I can remember as a child watching my grandmother (Mammaw) pull bundles of letters tied with ribbon or held together with rubber bands from her musty trunk. She would untie them and smooth them with her purple-veined hands. Then she would hold them up to the light that filtered through the nearby lace curtains, and tipping her bifocals to her advantage, she would read aloud the names printed in the left-hand corners, until she found the one she wanted me to hear. Her eyes would fill with distinct pleasure as she read details that folks had chosen to share, making her feel once again connected with them.

Yes, times have changed, but our need to be plugged in to each other has not. God purposed that we be in relationship from the beginning, for our good. He knew we would need each other. And when we isolate and unplug from others, our thinking becomes myopic, our needs become magnified, and past offenses mount up to inflict fresh pain.

It is not always easy to endure people even though "we are one." They can get on our nerve endings with their cleats of insensitivity, exposing our intolerance and revealing their humanity. But people also confirm our strengths and support us in our weaknesses. And there is something about when we invest in others, in God's generous economy, that we are equally blessed. Holy reciprocity.

Author and friend Ian Cron caught my attention recently during a luncheon visit when he remarked, "Remember, don't mistake connection for intimacy." (Pause and think on that.)

Just because we are friends with a person doesn't mean we've shared our story, whispered our dreams, or admitted our faults. Recently a new friend shared a hurtful event in her life with me. She was wary lest I think less of her. I was moved by the depth of her pain, the judgment she endured, and the sorrow that remained hers as she lived out of the aftermath of her choices. When we parted company, I felt honored to have been entrusted with that part of her story. I felt as though our friendship had deepened, that trust had been established, and I felt connected to her.

So how do we plug in to people? Do we run around telling people our deepest secrets and our tenderest dreams? No. Let me say that again. No. Just for clarity—no, no, no. Not everyone is equipped to bear the privacy of others. They may not know how to guard their own hearts, much less ours. And those who lack a sense of who they are aren't aware of how vital personal stories are to another's identity.

We are hurt and feel betrayed when someone divulges something we've entrusted them with, yet I wonder if it is that we have not been discerning or if our need to be known hasn't driven us to say more than we should have to those within earshot? We tend to confide in those with whom we spend the most time, and they tend to be at similar levels of maturity as ourselves. I find it's important to seek out those who have come further along to confide in. That's not to say that in their humanity they will not let us down—or we them. Disappointment, forgiveness, and resolve are all important paths to maturity. We all have the opportunity to enter those portals and come out the other side more discerning and more trustworthy.

Remember Samson? He was a fellow full of divine strength who trusted Delilah with his secret. At first he did not tell her the truth when she prodded him, but instead he fed her false information, and Delilah proved untrustworthy with his private information every time. She squealed to his enemies. Yet Samson, knowing she couldn't be trusted, eventually revealed to her that his hair must never be cut or his strength would be depleted.

Oh, Samson, honey, why did you do that? You were mentally astute enough to test Delilah and yet foolish enough to tell her the key to your God-given strength anyway. I can't imagine how you felt when your eyes were gouged out, your hair cut off, and heavy chains draped around your now weakened frame.

My friend Andy Andrews wrote on Twitter, "Trust a person the first time when they say who they are by their actions. It will save you grief later." I thought, *That's brilliant advice*, and I hurried to write it down.

Samson needed an iPhone, a Twitter account, and he needed to follow Andy.

Speaking of the Internet, remember whatever you send out into cyberspace endures. Be sure in your desire to connect with others you don't say things you'll regret or that can be used against you at a later date. Everyone out there is not, not, not your friend. Traverse the unforgiving terrain carefully.

And may I just caution those of you eager for romance: do not establish an intimate relationship online with someone you have not actually met. A casual friendship is one thing, but a healthy love connection needs face-to-face, voice-to-ear, eye-to-action, and some daily involvement for a "real" relationship to grow. Online distance involves a disconnect that leaves a lot of important details uncertain. A relative of mine met and married a lovely young woman he met online, but they visited each other in person on a number of occasions to find out if what they thought about each other was true. The Internet can be the perfect cover for those who don't dare reveal themselves or their motives, and they use cyberspace to victimize naive, needy, lonely people.

Yep, it takes more than a cord and an outlet to build lasting relationships. Les and I have been married more than forty-eight years, and we have found it takes humor, forgiveness, flexibility, and individual faith.

None of us wants a Samson result where we are blinded, shackled, and weakened because we didn't power up from the right Outlet. So here's my offering: Plug in to God's Word—it will grow you in discernment. Plug in to others discerningly—it will enlarge your heart. Plug in to reality because truth will lead to liberty.

2

Our Very Own "Get out of Jail Free" Card

. . . .

Lisa Harper

*I*t was a totally normal Sunday. There I was, loitering in the church foyer between worship services, daydreaming about where to go for lunch and how many extra miles I'd have to run if I ate the carbohydrates I was craving, when a woman with flyaway brown hair rushed up beside me. She grabbed my arm and whispered enthusiastically, "I'm so glad you've started teaching our Bible study! Before you came, all the leaders were blonde and thin and perfect looking, but when you came I finally felt comfortable and . . . and . . ." The second she realized how left-handed her compliment had come out, she stammered awkwardly. Then she scurried off as quickly as she'd come upon me, but I couldn't help grinning in her wake.

That church hallway encounter is probably the first time I've ever been delighted to be described as a not-thin, less-than-perfect-looking brunette because I've only recently begun to be completely comfortable in my own God-given skin. Even though I put my faith in Jesus Christ when I was a little girl, I spent decades way too concerned about what other people thought. The better part of my adolescence and young adulthood was spent trying to draw inside the "good Christian girl" lines superimposed by a conservative evangelical culture. I wore dresses and shiny shoes to church, I tried not to wiggle anything inappropriately when pop music was playing, and I never, ever cussed in public. I did my very best to *look* spiritual.

And while I'm certainly not advocating pelvic-dominant dance moves or the casual use of expletives, I did ultimately begin to ponder the juxtaposition between Jesus' words in the gospel of John—"So if the Son sets you free, you will be free indeed" (John 8:36 NIV)—and the people-pleasing, performance-oriented posture of my own life. I began to wonder what Jesus thought about all the superficial, unnecessary junk I lugged around and labeled spiritual. And, my yearning for the real liberty Jesus promised grew stronger and stronger. I began aching to experience what another woman did around two thousand years ago:

> One of the Pharisees asked Jesus to have dinner with him, so Jesus went to his home and sat down to eat. When a certain immoral woman from that city heard

he was eating there, she brought a beautiful alabaster jar filled with expensive perfume. Then she knelt behind him at his feet, weeping. Her tears fell on his feet, and she wiped them off with her hair. Then she kept kissing his feet and putting perfume on them.

When the Pharisee who had invited him saw this, he said to himself, "If this man were a prophet, he would know what kind of woman is touching him. She's a sinner!"

Then Jesus answered his thoughts. "Simon," he said to the Pharisee, "I have something to say to you."

"Go ahead, Teacher," Simon replied.

Then Jesus told him this story: "A man loaned money to two people—500 pieces of silver to one and 50 pieces to the other. But neither of them could repay him, so he kindly forgave them both, canceling their debts. Who do you suppose loved him more after that?"

Simon answered, "I suppose the one for whom he canceled the larger debt."

"That's right," Jesus said. Then he turned to the woman and said to Simon, "Look at this woman kneeling here. When I entered your home, you didn't offer me water to wash the dust from my feet, but she has washed them with her tears and wiped them with her hair. You didn't greet me with a kiss, but from the time I first came in, she has not stopped kissing my feet. You neglected the courtesy of olive oil to anoint my head, but she has anointed my feet with rare perfume.

"I tell you, her sins—and they are many—have been forgiven, so she has shown me much love. But a person who is forgiven little shows only little love." (Luke 7:36–47 NLT)

This woman was so preoccupied with worshipping Jesus that she didn't stop to think what the Pharisees watching her intimate gesture might think. She was so wholly undone by his mercy that she broke free from the chains of spiritual propriety. It didn't matter what anyone else thought; all that mattered to her was expressing her gratitude for his amazing grace. Her abandon illustrates how personal *freedom* is directly proportionate to our comprehension of divine *forgiveness*. Authentic emancipation comes with giving up our attempts to justify ourselves and leaning—I mean *really* leaning, putting all our weight—on the fact that God's mercy is big enough to redeem the bad things we've done and the bad things that have been done to us.

Have you ever wondered what it would feel like to be that uninhibited? That unconcerned about whether anyone else approves of your actions as long as the Savior is smiling? How incredible would it be to walk through the rest of our lives with a kick in our step even though our hearts are dotted with old scars and some of us have thighs that rub together? As radical as that sounds, I know beyond a shadow of a doubt that this kind of liberty is possible. I know because of my own ongoing liberation story, because of the ancient liberation stories I read in Scripture, and because of the current liberation stories I get to figuratively read on the road.

For instance, a woman approached me recently at a Women of Faith conference. She was well dressed and well-spoken, probably about my age. She leaned in close, looked down at her feet, and whispered, "I've been walking in shame for thirty years. I've known Jesus since I was a little girl, but I was sexually molested from the time I was eight until I was thirteen by my uncle, and it left me pretty damaged. I haven't felt pretty or wanted or clean since." After a considerable pause, she took a half step backward and looked up, staring intently into my eyes. Then she took a deep breath and declared with trembling, newfound confidence, "But tonight I sensed God saying, 'You're beautiful to me,' and I feel like I've taken my first step toward finally being free." We hugged for a minute or two, and the whole while she kept saying softly, "God loves me! God loves me! God loves me!" I thought, *Yes, he does. Yes, he does. Yes, he does,* long after she walked away.

I had a similar conversation in a church on the outskirts of Chicago not long ago. At that particular event, I taught from Matthew 1, focusing on how our heavenly Father graciously wove women with checkered pasts— chicks like Rahab, who spent time as a working girl in the red-light district, and Bathsheba, who got jiggy with King David while she was still married to a deployed soldier named Uriah—into the literal family tree of our Messiah and how their inclusion illustrates the fact that perfection isn't a prerequisite for relationship with God. At the end of the day, a beautiful young woman came up and told me it was the first time she'd been inside a sanctuary in more than four years. Then she began to share her story with the words, "I've been Bathsheba." She went on to describe the paralyzing guilt that accompanied her decision to sleep with a man she wasn't married to and how she'd allowed it to separate her from Jesus, her family, and her friends. She also held my gaze when she said firmly, "But today I was reminded that no sin is more powerful than God's forgiveness." She winked before adding, "I'll be back here tomorrow."

Our Creator-Redeemer's lavish affection and forgiveness really do set captives free. Whether your prison bars have been cemented in place by guilt, shame, pain, or by a mortar made up of all three, they cannot withstand the power of Christ's love. Emotional and spiritual jailbreak is inevitable when we move toward Jesus!

"The Lord God has put his Spirit in me, because the Lord has appointed me to tell the good news to the poor. He has sent me to comfort those whose hearts are broken, to tell the captives they are free, and to tell the prisoners they are released" (Isaiah 61:1 NCV).

3

Searching

· · · · · · · · · · · ·

Marilyn Meberg

*E*bony is in search of something beyond what he's experiencing. I assume that is what motivates my neighbor's darling little black cocker spaniel to continually dig new holes under the fence in order to gain access to my backyard. So far, Ebony has dug seven successful holes only to have them filled by his "mama," who puts a cement paving stone in each hole. Undeterred, Ebony simply moves several feet down the fence line and digs a new hole.

It would be flattering to think his relentless digging has something to do with my personal magnetism. But in all reality, I think Ebony's behavior springs from a deeper root.

At first I thought he was simply bored. I considered the possibility that he needed more frequent walks. Then it dawned on me: Ebony is simply searching for an escape from his yard. I wondered what might possibly be in my yard that he thinks would be better than his. Another dawning: perhaps it's the absence of the "other" dog who lives at Ebony's house and shares his yard. The other dog is some kind of fluffy-white-hybrid prone to incessant excitability over anything that moves slightly: the air, a fly, a blade of grass, or—mercy—another dog walking the path outside his gate.

The movement of a fly produces nervous yapping, but the movement of another dog produces wildly frenetic barking and racing from one end of the yard to the other. Only when the foreign dog has walked out of view does fluffy-white-hybrid drop into a heap of agitated exhaustion.

In all of this, Ebony is only an observer, not a participant. I'm assuming his tolerance of the environmental chaos fluffy-white-hybrid produces came to an abrupt end. Perhaps escape appeared to be his only option; thus the digging began. What Ebony had not taken into consideration is that fluffy-white-hybrid's chaos drifted over into my backyard as well.

Sometimes, like Ebony, something can snap in all of us as we consider our own environmental chaos. We suddenly say, "Okay . . . enough is enough . . . I am out of here." The question is, "Where am I going in order to escape this chaos?"

I was tempted to cup Ebony's little fur face in my

hand and say, "Baby . . . fluffy-white-hybrid is disturbing my tranquility also. You have not improved your environment by sitting next to my chair while I have tea and toast. We can both hear and see fluffy-white-hybrid. I can go into my house, but you, sweetheart, cannot come into my house. I am not your mama." I had to leave the challenge with him.

I am not without empathy for Ebony. I well remember my first job at the age of eighteen when something snapped in me and I said, "Okay. Enough is enough. I am out of here." I was working as a clerk-typist the summer after graduating from high school. I was fortunate to have the job because I would leave in the fall for college; I needed the money. But after two weeks, I announced to my father that I was going to quit. I told him there was so much filth and profanity in the office that I was not only shocked but also totally offended. I told Dad that no believer in Jesus should have to experience the contamination of that office, and I'd decided I had no option but to get out of the environment.

My father gave me a quiet, steady stare and then said, "No, Marilyn, you are not going to quit. Being a preacher's kid, you've been sheltered from the real world. That's not good for you. Jesus mixed with those who needed him— sinners. So now, honey, you get off your spiritual high horse and mix it up with those office people. We are called to be 'a light in a darkened world.' Go back tomorrow and start shining."

I was stunned by his words. I was sure he would agree that I needed protection from office filth. I was quiet all evening as his words began to make sense to me. I went back the next morning with a new perspective. I restrained myself from announcing to everyone that they were a bunch of sinners and that I was called to be a light in their filthy darkness. Ultimately I was received by them and even liked. One of the women, the most profane, started calling me "Purity," but she was also the one who began to seek me out during coffee breaks and tell me about her life. I was only eighteen and stunned to learn how she had made such a mess of things in thirty-four years. When I told her during one morning break that she needed Jesus she scoffed, lit a cigarette, and said, "Sure, sure, purity." On my last day, she gave me a bottle of perfume called Tigress, said I needed to develop my animal side, and included a card that said she'd miss me. I have no idea if she ever took my suggestion of Jesus-in-her-life seriously. I'll probably never know. Jesus knows.

Sometimes the God of the universe tells us to stay put, to live in the chaos of the environment because there is a reason we are there. Perhaps that reason is simply to be a light in someone's dark world, a light divinely placed for someone known and loved by God.

Ephesians 5:8 tells us that now we are full of light from the Lord, and our behavior should show it. Sometimes being a light means using words; sometimes it means casting an unconditional love glow that neither affirms or condemns—it just glows.

All this was far too complicated to explain to Ebony. Besides, I realized when I found him happily trotting around the neighborhood that he had far more in mind than casting an unconditional love glow for fluffy-white-hybrid. My last dawning: he was searching for freedom. That's what Ebony had wanted all along: freedom. But freedom from what? Apparently freedom not only from fluffy-white-hybrid but also from the confines of a yard that no longer held challenges for his active little cocker spaniel mind. If he had been able to explain his heart to me as I scooped him up for the return ride back to his yard and his own mama, I think he might have said, "Miss Marilyn, I realize my water bowl is always full and my food bowl never runs empty. I appreciate that I have a big, cuddly dog pillow with my name etched in bright red. I also like the fact that my house is air-conditioned, and I don't have to sit or stand in the heat of the Texas sun; I can go in and out of the doggy door anytime I choose. I want you to know I am not an ungrateful dog. But there are times when I want more. More of what? I don't really know, but surely there's more to life than this. There's too much sameness. I need variety. There must be places I can go, other dogs I can meet, and maybe even beaches where I can run. I'd like to race along a beach shoreline until I drop from happy exhaustion. Life's too short to just live in the backyard until I can't dig anymore. Ya know what I'm sayin'?" Wow. Do I ever, you darling little fur face. You are shining an encouraging light into my soul.

There are times when I, too, need to dig my way out of sameness, out of routine and narrow thoughts. I need to extend my borders to include new people, new ways of thinking, and more creative ways of being. I, too, need freedom from sameness. Maybe I need to work at a homeless shelter, deliver meals on wheels, volunteer to hold babies at a medical center, or become involved in a prison ministry.

I am indebted to Patsy Clairmont for an Old Testament verse that proved to be an inspiration as well as a motivator to her and, now, to me. God said to his people in Deuteronomy 1:6–7, "You have stayed at this mountain long enough. It is time to break camp and move on" (NLT).

There are instances when God calls us to stay put, to be a light in the darkness. But there are times when he says "Okay now—let's move on."

Maybe you are in a phase of life when the restlessness you are experiencing is a nudge from God. It is meant to move you out of sameness, to experience the freedom of new challenges. David said in Psalm 119:32, "Thou shalt enlarge my heart" (KJV). We can trust God's enlargement of our heart because he says, "I know the plans I have for you. . . . They are plans for good and not for disaster, to give you a future and a hope" (Jeremiah 29:11 NLT).

I experience a lot of interior freedom with that kind of encouragement. It makes me feel I've no need to dig furtively anymore. Oh, and by the way, if you happen to see Ebony trotting about, tell him Mama's got new kibble in the food bowl.

4

Tearing Down Walls

. . . .

Mary Graham

g reat surprises are a wonderful part of life, and usually, they live with us long after the moment. That's what I experienced in November of 2009. At first I thought it was just a huge disappointment.

The surprise was actually the continuation of a plan that had unfolded years before. In the early 1990s, I was part of a team that traveled to the former Soviet Union for ministry to university students. There were various people who traveled with us, but my dear friend Patty Burgin and I always traveled together. In fact, we traveled much of the world together, enjoying student ministry and having our share of adventure. Since then, we've laughed and talked about those days whenever and however our paths have crossed.

Last year I had an opportunity to have a long, leisurely dinner with Patty in Seattle, where she now lives. During that evening, we talked about being in Leningrad in 1989 when the Wall in East Berlin came down, a significant event that ultimately crushed communism in eastern Europe. We laughed about how the students there told us they'd heard this great news while listening to BBC on their shortwave radios. Such radios were illegal in the Soviet Union at the time, but some students managed to find a way to get them in order to hear news from the outside world. We assured them they must have misunderstood something. However, as soon as we arrived at the train station in Helsinki (our first stop in the Western world), there were newspapers plastered everywhere announcing the Wall had indeed come down and people in the East were free. Everyone was rejoicing. In essence, communism, with its restrictive control, was dead. We were stunned but knew it was "amazing grace" for those people and the world.

Fast-forward through twenty years of freedom in not only Russia but also the whole Communist Bloc in eastern Europe, and what we saw was indeed a miracle. As we reminisced, Patty looked at me over our dessert and said with all the spark and spontaneity I've seen in her thousands of times in the past, "Let's go to St. Petersburg in November for the twentieth anniversary of the Wall coming down." As spontaneously as she said it, I responded with great enthusiasm. I hadn't traveled with Patty for years, nor had I been on a trip like this, and yet it seemed as natural and right as if she'd said, "Let's do lunch."

Two months later, I arrived at the Dallas airport, ready to fly to Frankfurt, where Patty and I would connect and fly immediately to St. Petersburg. That was the plan. Then the unbelievable happened.

The airline agent said, "Miss Graham, you need a visa for Russia." I responded, "Of course. It's right here." "Where?" she asked. As I looked through my paperwork, I discovered there was no visa. I phoned my office and, after a few calls, realized it wasn't there, or anywhere. It had not been secured. I have no idea how we missed it, but I didn't have it, and there is no way to travel into Russia without a tourist visa issued by their government and ours. Sweet Lara Dulaney, one of our vice presidents, said, "I'll go to Houston and get one for you!"

Of course there was no time for that. My plane to Frankfurt was leaving in three hours. Patty's plane was to leave Seattle shortly after mine, so I called her. We were both deeply disappointed. I had the additional angst of feeling my own stupidity for not checking earlier. Patty and I talked, prayed, and hung up the phone. Five minutes later, while I was still standing near the counter in stunned silence, she called back with a brilliant Plan B: "Let's go to Berlin," Patty said. "We'll fly to Frankfurt, then take a train to Berlin. I'm sure they'll be commemorating the anniversary in Berlin. Maybe even more than in Russia!"

So, I went back to the agent, changed my ticket, and made my way to Frankfurt. I felt foolish for making such a mistake, disappointed I wouldn't get to go to Russia, and very sad and embarrassed that I'd let Patty down. Luci Swindoll is fond of saying, "I felt so low I could have put on a top hat and walked under a duck."

But as I took my sad feelings with me on the plane that day, there was one thing I didn't know. Berlin on November 9, 2009, was the best place on the planet to be. In fact, it was better than anyone could have ever imagined. God, who loves putting his people in the right place at the right time, knew. Everyone in the world was watching the Berlin festivities that day. Berlin was hosting the world of political leaders who were commemorating twenty years of freedom in eastern Europe. Who knew? Patty and I certainly didn't.

So in Frankfurt, instead of changing planes to fly to St. Petersburg, Patty and I boarded a train to Berlin. One of the stops was a city where Patty has a friend, so we stopped, had dinner, spent the night, walked around in the adorable village the next morning, and hopped back on the train for Berlin. It was delightful.

When we arrived in Berlin, it was hustle and bustle everywhere as plans for the festivities for the big day were unfolding and the dignitaries were arriving. Patty and I walked the streets, had leisurely meals, and lingered over coffee. We caught up on the last twenty years and laughed and cried over all we had experienced together as much younger women traipsing around the world together, sharing the love of God with college students on almost every continent and in every language. In those days, we had traveled on a "shoestring," and what we lacked in security and comfort, we made up for in adventure. It was as if no time had passed. And *then*, the morning of November 9, we made our way to the very place the Wall had been erected. Here's what the Associated Press said about that day in Berlin:

> Thousands of cheering Germans re-enacted the electrifying moment the Berlin Wall came crashing down—toppling 1,000 graffiti-adorned 8-foot-tall dominoes that tumbled along the route of the now vanished Cold War icon, celebrating 20 years of freedom from separation and fear. The spectacle—billed by organizers as a metaphor for the way the real wall came down 20 years ago Monday and the resulting fall of communist countries in eastern Europe—was one of several events to mark the anniversary and celebrate the profound change it had not only in Germany, but Europe and the world.

We walked back and forth all day, studying those tall "dominoes" and talking for hours about freedom, life, hope, change, and God. We sat in little cafés and visited with people who told us in broken English about their lives behind the wall in East Berlin. We remembered our own President Reagan, who had visited Berlin during his tenure and in a 1987 speech said those famous words, "Mr. Gorbechev, *tear down this wall!*" We celebrated being Americans living in a land of freedom.

It was one perfect day, and I was with someone I love dearly and with whom I have shared some of life's best, most exhilarating moments. And I almost missed it. I almost missed it because I didn't know enough to go there. I had no idea that it was the spot where I needed to be on that very day. And Patty was the one I would have wanted to share it with, had I known.

That's what happens when we trust God with everything. He takes our plans, and even when we feel disappointed because he changes them, we trust. We follow. And he works it all out for our good.

I've seen that happen more times than I can remember. And many of those have been while traveling with Patty. We had a wonderful week together in Berlin, reminiscing about the old, enjoying the new, and exploring each other's growth and development for the first time in years. It was . . . perfect. Who knew? God. Romans 8:28 can get us through life without worry or fear: "And we know that all things work together for good to those who love God, to those who are the called according to His purpose" (NKJV).

I'm an organizer, and I like to be in charge of things. My preference is to make a plan, work it all out in my head, team with the right people, and make it happen. That is the way God wired me. But I have to remember, my preference is not always God's plan. In my walk of faith, I'm often challenged when things don't go the way I imagined they should. I usually feel confident in my plans, but God's ways are infinitely higher, better, and much richer than my own. Even when, or maybe especially when, I'm surprised by his plan. He delights in leading us every step of the way. His way.

5

Filled with Life

....

Luci Swindoll

For ten years I couldn't breathe. Or, better said, I had trouble breathing. I didn't know it, of course, or I would have tried to change it. I just knew I was tired all the time, sleepy more often than not, and undependable when it came to being alert at important times. During that ten-year period, I was working at my day job, traveling on weekends, and trying to get eight hours of sleep at night. None of it was without moments of drama.

I well remember driving down the street, falling asleep at the wheel, and bumping into the car in front of me at a stoplight. It was a little "bump," but noticeable and disconcerting to say the least. But there were times that were much more troublesome than that. For example, I'd be scheduled to speak at three o'clock in the afternoon, and when my introduction was over, someone had to tap me on the arm or shoulder to wake me up so I could go to the podium and begin my message. There were also many times I'd be sitting at the computer typing a letter; my head would slump, and my hand would fall on the Enter key, taking the note w-a-y down the page (or pages). I would fall sound asleep, only to awaken a couple minutes later with a gigantic space between my last typed line and several rows of *zzzzzzzzzzzzzzz's*, literally.

Back in the mid-1990s, when I first started speaking with Women of Faith, more often than not I traveled with one of two friends, who helped with my books on the concourse, so we'd be rooming together at various hotels. They told me (kindly, of course) that my snoring was so loud, it often kept them awake. Even though they were extremely sweet about it, they let me know I snored, and not only that, I held my breath. For long periods of time. And it scared them. *Oh my gosh!* I had no idea that was going on. They added, "You not only hold your breath, Luci, but you gasp for breath, and we have the feeling you're going to die. It really scares us. Maybe you should see a doctor and check out what's wrong. We'll let you hold your breath if you want to, but you can't die." We'd laugh about it from time to time, but down deep inside, I knew I had to address the problem. And the sooner, the better.

The tipping point came one day when I was in a bookstore with Mary Graham, and she found the words *sleep apnea* in an encyclopedia and read me the definition:

A common disorder that affects more than 18 million people in the United States. In many of these people, the condition is undiagnosed; Obstructive Sleep Apnea, (OSA) takes its name from the Greek word *apnea*, which means "without breath." People with sleep apnea literally stop breathing repeatedly during their sleep often for a minute or longer and as many as hundreds of times during a single night.

For the first time in months, I woke up. The word *apnea* caught my attention. It was then I decided to make arrangements to spend the night at a sleep clinic near my home and have this problem checked out, just to see how serious it really was. A technician attached electrodes to several places on my head and body, with wires running to an adjacent room. In that room were monitors that recorded her findings:

> I slept 125 minutes and awakened 123 times during those minutes.
> I then slept 102 minutes, and awakened 71 times.
> I held my breath many times, the longest of which was 43 seconds.

It was determined I had 83 percent OSA. In other words, I had severe sleep apnea.

After this diagnosis was made and during that same

night, the technician strapped a sleep apnea CPAP (Continuous Positive Airway Pressure) unit onto my face, and I went sound asleep for five hours without ever opening my mouth, snoring, holding my breath, or awakening myself. It was the first *good* sleep I had had in maybe ten years. Needless to say, I was beside myself when I awakened. I vividly remember opening my eyes in that clinic and thinking, *So this is what it feels like to be free . . . to be "out of prison."* I can't adequately describe the joy that was mine that morning.

For weeks after that sleep clinic test, every time I answered the phone, I didn't say "Hello," I just sang, "This joy that I have; the world didn't give it to me. Oh no! No! This joy that I have . . ." (I'm sure my friends were thrilled about the resolution of my problem but, in time, longed for a simple, "Hello?") That test was done twelve years ago, and to this day I go everywhere with that CPAP unit. I've named it Dr. Lecter, from *Silence of the Lambs,* because one has the illusion that it's going to eat one's face during the night. But instead of that, it does the opposite. It enables me to breathe. Sleep. Rest. I didn't know how enslaved I was until this gadget filled me with life.

And the whole thing has become really quite funny. All my Women of Faith traveling companions know my CPAP unit as "Dr. Lecter," and everybody calls it that. On a plane, I usually put it in the overhead compartment above my seat, and if my friends are sitting nearby and we're getting ready to disembark upon landing, it's not unusual to hear one (or several) of them shout from her seat, "Who has Dr. Lecter?"

Freedom comes in many forms, doesn't it? But there are issues in life apart from which we don't enjoy freedom. For some, there are struggles with addiction that rob them of their freedom. Others are caught up with distractions that keep them from being free. I had a condition that kept me in bondage, and I didn't even know it. Something very real kept me from the freedom to live naturally, and I had no idea. I didn't even know there was a problem until I experienced dramatic change. Scripture teaches us that God "gives to His beloved even in his sleep" (Psalm 127:2 NASB), and that's certainly what he did for me. He filled my lungs with breath and, thus, new life from him.

Physically, I wasn't "free," and it had an impact on every facet of my life. The same can be true if we're not free emotionally, personally, financially. We can be a slave to something that controls us like an unwelcome, unwanted master. "It is for freedom that Christ has set us free" (Galatians 5:1 NIV). I know some well-meaning, hard-working, wonderful people who are "enslaved" financially. They're bound to misery in many ways because their finances are out of control. I have friends who have talked about an "emotional" bondage in an unhealthy relationship. I believe God wants to set us free from whatever kills, steals, or destroys our sense of well-being. Sometimes we need to take the first step toward that freedom. I'm sure you have heard or read the quote "Freedom isn't free."

To me, the most difficult bondage from which we must cut ourselves loose is the bondage of legalism. When Christ paid the ultimate price for our freedom on the cross, he made it possible to live a life of liberty in grace. And what that means is freedom from worry, remorse, fear, shame, and guilt. What an appealing gift he offers—and there are no strings attached. If we believe that, accept the truth of it, live like we mean it in all our waking moments, I can assure you, freedom will invade our lives. The apostle Paul encourages us to use our freedom "to serve one another in love; that's how freedom grows" (Galatians 5:14 MSG).

6

Steps for Freedom

Lisa Whelchel

There was a time when I was tempted in an area that I thought was behind me. It came out of the blue and started with a dream. I woke up the next morning and said to myself, "Where did that come from?" While I knew it came straight from the pit, I was surprised that my subconscious let it get through to my dream life. From that point on, old feelings began to resurface in an area that I had been successful at subduing for years. I didn't want the feelings, but they grew stronger and stronger.

The morning after that dream, the topic of my Bible study was obedience. In the response area, the author wrote, "Is there anything—even the tiniest thing—that you know God is asking of you, and yet you've hesitated?" I knew there wasn't any outright disobedience that I was aware of in my life, but I also knew I was planning a step in the wrong direction. I prayed for strength to resist, and then I wrote the following prayer in my journal:

Psalm 119:112—"I have inclined my heart to perform Your statutes forever, to the very end." Dear Lord, thank you for this struggle of obedience I am facing. Thank you for giving me an opportunity to choose you over myself. I resolve in my heart to obey you and resist temptation. I will not _____ [do the thing I was planning to do]. Now, Lord, I confess that I need your help. I cannot obey in my own strength. Be my Defender and my Deliverer. You are able to deliver the godly from temptation. Thank you for that. I will give you all the praise for the victory. Help me to walk in obedience with every step. Have mercy on me. I want to choose you. Help me. Give me strength and mercy when I am weak. Battle the forces of darkness on my behalf because of your goodness. I am your child and servant, and I look to you to be bigger than me and take care of me. Thank you, Father.

I made it through the day, and I followed through on my commitment not to take that step in the wrong direction. I was so glad I had made the commitment to the Lord in that moment of strength in the morning and had written it down, or I know I would have stumbled because the feelings, impulses, and compulsions grew stronger, not weaker. The best way to describe it is that a battle was raging between my feelings and my mind, my soul and my spirit, lies and the truth. It was downright oppressive and annoying. I didn't want these feelings. I had rejected them. Why were they still pressing in on me?

During a time of quiet, I cried out to the Lord. I confessed that I was not strong enough to fight these feelings. All I could do was run to him as my Shelter and Strong Tower and trust him to win the battle for me. Three more days, and this war raged on. I made choices in moments of strength not to let the enemy encroach even an inch by giving in to choices that appeared innocent on the outside but I knew were compromises. I did not "feed" the feelings; rather, I tried to take every thought captive to the obedience of Christ Jesus. I entered into worship often, asking God to use my praises as a weapon of warfare to drive back the oppressive spirit.

But mostly, I rested in the care of my heavenly Father and depended on him to defend me. I knew he wasn't mad at me for struggling in this area. I sensed that he wasn't upset that I wasn't able to overcome this in my own strength. Instead, I felt as though he took pleasure in knowing that I was counting on him to get me through this.

One night, in the middle of this battle, I had another dream. There was a dog attacking me. At first, I tried to fight back. I yelled at him and tried to bite him myself. That only made him madder, and it didn't stop him; he kept growling and snapping. Then I simply started to walk away from the dog, yet the dog did not chase me. Instead, he stood still and started yelping and crying because I was walking away, and he couldn't bite me anymore. He was thoroughly frustrated and apparently not allowed to follow me. He could only hurt me if I was close enough for him to reach me.

This dream reminded me of the verse James 4:7, "Submit yourselves therefore to God. Resist the devil, and he will flee from you" (ESV). Over the previous few days, I hadn't really engaged in any major "spiritual warfare," per se. Mostly, I had submitted my weakness honestly to God and had done my best to resist the devil's promptings.

After a few days of relentless battle, the oppression and temptation simply lifted. The feelings were gone. I could see clearly again. I felt like my old self again. I was overwhelmed with thanksgiving. I knew I had not won this battle, but the Lord had won it for me. I had been weak and had contemplated sinning against my heavenly Father; but I cried out to him, and he heard me and delivered me.

God doesn't want us to beat ourselves up with guilt because we have not been able to overcome certain temptations. Yes, there are some wise steps we can take, but deliverance ultimately comes from the Lord, not by gritting our teeth and vowing to do better next time.

Even so, I have learned there are some steps I can take to partner with the Lord as he sets me free. These are a few things I've learned that help when I find myself getting entangled with sin:

- "If we confess our sins, he is faithful and just to forgive us our sins and to cleanse us from all unrighteousness" (1 John 1:9 ESV).

Confess to the Lord—be honest with the Lord. Don't make excuses or rationalize. Shine the light on the ugliest parts in the deepest recesses of my mind and heart. Confess my weakness; even confess any desire I have to continue in the sin.

- "Therefore, confess your sins to one another and pray for one another, that you may be healed. The prayer of a righteous person has great power as it is working" (James 5:16 ESV).

Confess to a trusted friend or mentor—I have learned to be careful with this one. I must use wisdom in choosing a safe friend. It needs to be someone I know will not judge me, but who also won't blow this off as "no big deal." There is great power to break bondage by simply confessing it and bringing it out into the light, not to mention the prayer support I can also receive!

- "Sanctify them in the truth; your word is truth" (John 17:17 ESV).

Read my Bible—feed my spirit Truth to war against the lies that are floating around in my head.

- "The weapons we fight with are not the weapons of the world. On the contrary, they have divine power to demolish strongholds. We demolish arguments and every pretension that sets itself up against the knowledge of God, and we take captive every thought to make it obedient to Christ" (2 Corinthians 10:4–5 NIV).

Guard my mind: I have learned the importance of paying attention to what I'm thinking about. If I can take every thought captive in my mind, rather than dwelling on it and thinking about it, then I'll have a better chance at resisting the temptation in action.

- "When the righteous cry for help, the LORD hears and delivers them out of all their troubles" (Psalm 34:17 ESV).

Cry out to the Lord—call on him in the middle of my struggle. As soon as I recognize the feelings or patterns, I call out to the Lord for help. It is important for me to be honest. "Lord, I'm doing it again, and I don't want to. Help me. Please forgive me and show me the escape route you have prepared for me out of this temptation. Give me the strength to walk away. I'm sorry, Lord. I don't want this. I want you and uncomplicated, unhindered fellowship and relationship with you. I choose you over this temptation. Please rescue me. Please deliver me. I am trusting in you."

I am so grateful that God's resurrection power is available to us to overcome temptation and walk in victory. I'm even more grateful that his crucifixion power is ours even when we are overwhelmed and stumble in failure. I love the fact that I am free in Christ even before I experience freedom in my flesh: "When you were slaves of sin, you were free in regard to righteousness" (Romans 6:20 ESV).

7

Freedom to Let the Plates Fall

. . . .

Sheila Walsh

"Are you tired? Worn out? Burned out on religion? Come to me. Get away with me and you'll recover your life. I'll show you how to take a real rest. Walk with me and work with me—watch how I do it. Learn the unforced rhythms of grace. I won't lay anything heavy or ill-fitting on you. Keep company with me and you'll learn to live freely and lightly."

—Matthew 11:28–30 MSG

I knew something was wrong when I said "Amen" and opened my eyes. I didn't expect applause; after all, it was a prayer, but neither did I expect the scrutiny of the entire prayer group intentionally focused on me.

"What?" I said.

"What was that?" Richard asked.

"It was a prayer," I replied indignantly. "You might not want it on a T-shirt, but it was still a prayer."

"For what?" he said.

"For India!" I answered, just a little put out by the question. "What do you think I'd be praying for in the 'Let's pray for India' prayer group?"

"Very nice," he said, "but this is the Alcoholics Anonymous group, and while you might want to argue that there's a fairly good chance that there are some alcoholics in India, your prayer seemed a little bit of a stretch."

"Oops, wrong day, wrong room," I said as I backed out the door.

Truth is, when I was in college I was in so many prayer groups that I often got them mixed up and ended up praying for the president of Compassion International in the Godly Women Seeking a Husband Group. If it existed, I felt obliged to join it. Most of the time, I was a good juggler; but every now and then, as you can see, I dropped a few balls.

I think I learned to juggle at five. By that age, I had come to the conclusion that if you perform well, people love you, and if you perform poorly, they do not. We learn to juggle for different reasons as children. It can be because no one notices us if we just sit there. It can be to reduce the tension in our home. For me, it was to deflect my father's violent mood swings when his brain injury took center stage. The conclusion I came to was that just being me would never cut it, so I learned to juggle. For a few years I was a juggler in search of a circus, and then one day, there it was! Those in charge of the circus called it "ministry," but I could smell the sawdust on the floor and the candy floss in the air, and I knew I was home.

The circus had different levels of performers, and for most of my juggling career I was on the B team. Those in the A team could keep so many balls in the air it was dazzling. The applause they received was deafening, and I felt happy just to be under the same big top. The only problem with juggling is that you rarely get to sit down and be quiet or hug someone or just goof off, because you have to concentrate or you'll drop something.

One day my arms got too tired, and I dropped a ball. I should have just kept going, but instead I tried to pick it up, and then I dropped another and another, and before I could get myself together, it was all over. I left the tent before anyone could ask me to go; I thought it would be easier for us all. I sat under the stars that night and looked up; they were beautiful. It was so quiet away from the noise of the circus, and it was then that I could hear something soft and sweet.

> *Softly and tenderly Jesus is calling,*
> *Calling for you and for me;*
> *See, on the portals He's waiting and watching,*
> *Watching for you and for me.*
> *Come home, come home,*
> *You who are weary come home;*

Earnestly, tenderly, Jesus is calling,
Calling, oh [juggler] come home.
—*"Softly and Tenderly Jesus Is Calling"*
Will Thompson, 1880

I wonder if that strikes a chord with you? Do you feel as if you spend your whole day keeping plates spinning in the air, with little time to breathe? I don't know if it is simply that, as women, we feel pressured to make sure that everyone else is taken care of or if it is knit into our genetic code. Whatever the reason, we women have bought into the whole multitasking performance show.

But there are deeper levels, apart from the picture we get indelibly stamped into our souls from our culture as to what a woman should be able to accomplish in any given day. When we have been wounded in childhood, we often feel as if we find our worth in what we *do* for others rather than in who we *are* in Christ. At times, our church culture can add fuel to that fire, rewarding those who over-volunteer. But the truth remains; Jesus calls us into relationship with him based on what he has finished, not on anything we bring to the table. If you are like me, it is easy to agree with that in print but hard to let it sink all the way into our hearts.

The day that I left the "circus," I found myself in a psychiatric ward, diagnosed with severe clinical depression. Quite a contrast from being a performer one day to being a patient the next, but I look back on that day in 1992 now as one of God's greatest gifts of mercy to my life. I will never forget the first conversation I had with the psychiatrist. He asked me a question: "Who are you?"

I thought the question was ridiculous, as I can read upside down enough to see that my name was at the top of his notepad, but I played along.

"Sheila Walsh," I replied.

"I didn't ask for your name," he said. "Who are you?"

Hmm, a trick question?

"I'm the co-host of *The 700 Club*," I said.

"No, Sheila, I didn't ask what you do; who are you?"

I sat for a few moments and let his question sink through the haze of where I had been living for a while.

"I don't know," I said with profound sadness.

"I know that," he replied, "and that's why you're here."

It was during that time that I began to come to grips with the truth that, for so long, I had found my value in what I could "do" for God and for others. It was a liberating humility that let me see that there is nothing I can do or say to make God love me more or less. It is just who he is.

I will never forget the day I left the hospital. I was crossing the parking lot to get to my car, and my doctor called out of his study window, "Sheila, who are you?"

I replied, "I am Sheila Walsh, daughter of the King of kings!"

Nothing less will do.

Nothing else will last.

I invite you to let the plates fall and come and let Jesus love you.

I'm not sure if I'm supposed to keep this a secret or not, but I just wanted you to know that there is life outside the circus—and it is very good.

8

Voice of a Savior

． ． ． ． ． ． ． ． ． ． ．

Mandisa

A regular part of my weekly routine is doing interviews. Typically, one day a week is set aside for speaking with radio DJs, newspaper reporters, and Internet site correspondents. I've heard my fair share of questions, ranging from the future of *American Idol* to the future of Christian music. But when the attention turns to my own albums, the question I always have a difficult time answering is, "Of all the songs you sing, which one is your favorite?" For me, that answer depends on what is currently happening in my life. Over the years, my answer has ranged from "My Deliverer" to "God Speaking" and everything in between. But if you were to ask me that question right now, I would tell you that the song "Voice of a Savior" from my debut album, *True Beauty*, holds a special place in my heart. It connects the dots from a universal struggle so many of us face, to the center of the real issue. Countless numbers of us turn to ill-fitting idols in an attempt to fill that God-sized hole inside of us. Like the song says, some turn to alcohol. Some turn to drugs. Some turn to fortune or another person. Me? I turn to food.

I used to naively think that I simply liked the way it tasted. I mean, truth be told, few don't enjoy the salty and buttery goodness of movie-theater popcorn. What person does not moan with excitement upon walking into a room filled with the aroma of freshly baked cookies? What warm-blooded American doesn't appreciate the sight of hot apple pie with melting vanilla ice cream and caramel on top? I guess what sets me apart from the average person who can appreciate those things and move on is that I have a hard time stopping once I've indulged. I am a compulsive overeater. I don't stop after one cookie. I don't even stop after three or four. I can eat an entire roll of easy-bake cookies all by myself in one sitting. Inhaling a dozen warm Krispy Kreme donuts all at once is not outside the realm of possibilities for me. For as long as I can remember, I have turned to food to make me feel good.

I don't remember when the mind shift began for me, but looking back at old pictures, I can see that something changed when I was roughly eight years old. It was around that age that my cheeks, hips, and thighs started to swell. Food was becoming an emotional filler for me. Never one to acknowledge or deal with my feelings, I made food my way of escape. And with my parents' divorce, my father's move from California to Texas, being molested as a child, and being raped as a teenager, I had a lot to escape from. Why manage the sorrow, anger, and fear when I could experience the fleeting joy that a double-cheeseburger meal could provide?

Lining up photos in chronological order reveals a progression of sizes, culminating with a super morbidly obese adult woman in her early thirties. I was at my highest weight in 2007 when I released my debut album. Night after night, I would sing about my identity not being wrapped up in my outward appearance. From the stage, I would share that God was teaching me that I did not have to look like the women on the magazine covers, music videos, and catwalks. Instead of allowing my mirror to define me, I would allow my Father to define me. First Peter 3 was my theme scripture: "Your beauty should not come from outward adornment, such as braided hair and the wearing of gold jewelry and fine clothes. Instead, it should be that of your inner self, the unfading beauty of a gentle and quiet spirit, which is of great worth in God's sight" (vv. 3–4 NIV).

While I unwaveringly believe that women should not get their beauty standards from society, I also see how I began to twist that scripture to mean something it was not intended for. I used that verse as my license to eat as much as I wanted because I am more than my body. Indeed, I *am* more than my body, but my body *is* the temple of the Holy Spirit. While I don't believe that God is concerned with how I look on the outside, I do think he's concerned with how I take care of the temple he resides in. I saw that very clearly when I began recording my second album.

I would stand in the recording studio, singing phrases like "I have been set free," "With You on my side I am victorious . . . You will deliver me," and "My Deliverer set me free from all that held me captive." As the words came out of my mouth, I ushered up a silent prayer asking God if these things were true. It was one thing to sing, "Take the shackles off my feet so I can dance." After all, that was a prayer asking God to set me free. It seemed like quite another thing to proclaim that I had already been set free. I didn't feel free. I felt bound—shackled, if you will. That was when I decided that if I was going to stand on a stage and tell others that God could set them free from anything, I had to allow him to set me free from what held me captive: my relationship with food.

I hired a personal trainer, began seeing a therapist who specialized in eating disorders, and changed my eating habits to include more fruits, vegetables, lean meats, and whole grains. By the time my album *Freedom* was released in March 2009, I had lost seventy-five pounds!

It wasn't necessarily a quick loss, but it was consistent. After *Freedom* was released, I continued with my journey and lost an additional ten pounds. Then something happened. I began to tire of exercising every day. I longed for my old familiar friends Wendy, the King of burgers, and

Jack (you know—the one who lives in a box). But more than anything, I was exhausted with crying, talking about how I felt, and coming to terms with my past. Life seemed so much easier living fat. It was comfortable. Like another story I know: "The Israelites said to them, 'If only we had died by the LORD's hand in Egypt! There we sat around pots of meat and ate all the food we wanted, but you have brought us out into this desert to starve this entire assembly to death'" (Exodus 16:3 NIV).

Like the Israelites who had been set free from Egyptian bondage, I began to glamorize my years of enslavement. I considered the days of sitting on my couch, ignoring my emotions, and binge eating whatever I desired as freedom. Giving in to this mind-set, I quickly gained ten pounds. And then of course, I was miserable. To add to it, my weight-loss success was so public. Stories about it were seen on the television show *Extra* and *US Weekly* and *People* magazines, not to mention countless Internet sites. People seemed less impressed with any Dove and Grammy award nominations and more impressed with how I had shed so much weight. But with the increasing numbers on the scale came an increase of shame. And with shame came the inclination to cover it up by eating. Those ten pounds I had gained eventually turned to twenty-five, which is where I am as I write this today. However, after a brief meltdown, I am learning to consider this a step on a journey, which is more important than the final destination.

If you, like me, have fought this fight with food for as long as you can recall, know that you are not alone. I am not one speaking to you as someone who has mastered it (can you tell that Philippians 3:13–14 is a favorite of mine?). I am simply coming to you as a fellow sister on this journey to be free. Truly free. Rick Warren recently said on Twitter, "Freedom is not the absence of limit. It is the power God graciously offers you to say yes to what's right and no to wrong."

This journey to freedom from a food-related stronghold is a physical, mental, emotional, and spiritual adventure.

Physical—I am not going to spend the rest of my life viewing a piece of bread as my enemy. I am learning the art of choosing foods that nourish me *and* that I enjoy. The diet business is a billion-dollar industry. For me, focusing on health is more important than a quick fix. Similarly, I don't have to be a body builder or marathon runner, but I do need to make physical activity a regular part of my life. Finding something I enjoy has made a huge difference for me. My Zumba class is like a big ole dance party! I burn hundreds of calories, and I have a good time doing it. Because I enjoy it, I am more likely to stick with it.

Mental—My friend Lysa TerKeurst wrote in her book *Made to Crave*, "I am a Jesus girl who can step on the scale and simply see an indication of how much my body weighs, not the worth of who I am" (Grand Rapids: Zondervan, 2010). On those Monday mornings, after two weeks of moving my body, eating foods that nourish me, and feeling my emotions, I will not allow the number on the scale to send me into a tailspin. I will choose to think about my weight as a journey to freedom, not merely a number to be attained.

Emotional—I believe that my weight gain is simply a symptom of a much deeper issue. Uncovering the root causes of my propensity to turn to food is as important a part of this journey as what I eat and how I move. My therapist and community of like-minded friends have been a tremendous help for me in this area. They love, pray for, and call me out on things that are contrary to my new, healthy lifestyle. For me, this is the most difficult part of the process. But it is necessary and crucial for my success.

Spiritual—Earlier I quoted from Exodus when speaking of the Israelites' yearning for Egypt. The very next verse says, "Then the LORD said to Moses, 'I will rain down bread from heaven for you. The people are to go out each day and gather enough for that day'" (Exodus 16:4 NIV). You see, God does not want me to worry about tomorrow. I must depend on him for my *daily* bread. Each day. One day at a time. Moreover, knowing that I don't have to walk this road by myself brings me great comfort. In moments of temptation, I have learned that my willpower alone will not help me through. Thankfully, God's power is limitless. Turning to him in prayer and audibly proclaiming scriptures have become a lifeline for me (my favorite is 1 Corinthians 10:13). I am allowing God to use this thorn in my flesh to draw me into a closer relationship with him. Offering my body to God has become a spiritual act of worship (Romans 12:1).

I don't know what tomorrow holds. But today I will choose to heed the voice of my Savior, who said in Luke 4:18, "The Spirit of the Lord is on Me, because . . . He has sent Me to proclaim freedom to the captives . . . to set free the oppressed" (HCSB).

Assurance

1

Going the Extra Mile

....

Luci Swindoll

*O*ne of my favorite memories happened in the strang-est setting. It was the last day of January 2010, and I was in Addis Ababa, Ethiopia, in a somewhat beat-up hotel bar, sitting with a group of seven people, when a woman walked in who was part of our traveling entourage but whom I had not yet met. Her name is Donna Galli. Donna and her husband, Jeff, had come from their home in Tonopah, Nevada, to Addis, on a different flight than Mary Graham and I, but our purpose for being there was the same—to meet the Ethiopian family whom Donna sup-ports through the work of the relief organization World Vision. One of the few available places in the hotel to gather was the bar, so we all dragged chairs around a little round table and began talking, telling our stories of how we got from America to Ethiopia . . . and why.

Donna is a bit hard to explain. Everything about her

speaks of love, generosity, sincerity, and honesty. It's not as though I don't know other people who have those traits, but this woman epitomizes each one. She's sixty years old, married with five children and nine grandchildren—a high school graduate, an accountant, and one who loves Women of Faith. She's attended our conferences for ten years. Donna is fun, enterprising, enthusiastic, and a strong believer in Jesus Christ. She'd give you the shirt off her back if you needed it.

Here's the story she told us that afternoon:

In 2002, Donna attended the *Irrepressible Hope* Women of Faith Conference in Sacramento, California. Mary was emceeing that weekend, and at one point, Donna heard her say, "If you sponsor a World Vision child, you will be able to help the whole family. You can make a difference for a lifetime." Moved by those words and God's Spirit, Donna went to the World Vision table at the break to look through the folders in hopes of finding "just the right child" to sponsor. A young girl from Ethiopia, Senayit Bedada, caught her attention. Senayit lived with her mother and five siblings in an Ethiopian village. "This girl had the saddest eyes," Donna said. "I put the picture down several times and walked away, but something kept bringing me back to it. Her eyes had no hope." Donna looked carefully at Senayit's face and found it irresistible. *I can't do everything*, she thought, *but I can do this*, so she signed up for that sponsorship, and "That's where my journey began."

A lot of people sponsor children and do a wonderful job of it. They write letters and send birthday greetings. They pray for those children and their families and the villages in which they live. But Donna? She did all that and more. She started writing Senayit, who responded to Donna's letters, so they established a wonderful, warm relationship through snail mail. Then Donna began writing Senayit's mother, Wosenee, encouraging her as a caretaker for all her children. In essence, Donna became the mentor for Wosenee. Donna sent packages to the family—eight to ten a month. If it fit in a box, she mailed it.

One day she called the World Vision office and learned she could do even more. "It started with a milk cow (with an ox thrown in), then a few chickens, three pregnant goats, another ox, more goats, a few sheep, an old donkey, then a younger donkey." I stopped her there and asked why two donkeys? "Because that first donkey wouldn't do his chores," she laughed. All the while this was going on, Donna was sending extra money through World Vision for clothes for Senayit and the other children—toys, school supplies, seeds, grain, fertilizer, corn, and beans. The giving never stopped. And know this: Donna is not a wealthy woman. She's just like you and me—working to make ends meet in her own family situation—but with a huge desire to go the extra mile, in *every* way possible.

As the months and years went by, Donna learned that the Bedada family lived in a tiny thatched roof hut, with all six of them sleeping on a dirt floor at night. When it rained, the water poured in through a leaky roof, and Wosenee was at her wit's end. With the help of World Vision, Donna sent money to build them a house and a corral for the animals. If that weren't enough, she ordered electricity to be run to every house in the village (at her monthly expense) so the children could do their homework by electric light instead of candlelight.

By the time we got to this part of the story, I was weeping, as was everyone at that table. It was the most marvelous account of generosity and goodness I had ever heard. I asked Donna how much she spends a year on this family, and Jeff said very quietly and humbly, "We don't keep track." Then I turned to him and asked, "Why does Donna do this, Jeff? What is her motive?"

"Well," he said, "I have a ministry of sending Bibles to Europe and she wanted her own ministry, so she chose this. She loves this family. Besides, it's fun." The next day, we met the World Vision staff in charge of the Bedada family and through whom Donna works to see that her money is spent in the manner she chooses. The leader of the group was Solomon, a tall, gentle man who loves his job. The staff had invited us to a "Coffee Celebration" under the trees that afternoon, and the minute we were seated around the coffee-roasting area, Donna pulled Solomon aside and asked, "How can I buy a progressive cow for the Bedadas?" And I'm thinking, *What in the world is a "progressive cow"?* Solomon and Donna had never met, but the minute that sentence came out of her mouth, he said to her with a big smile on his face, "I think you must be Donna Galli." What a fabulous, far-reaching reputation this wonderful woman has.

On February 2, Donna finally met Senayit face-to-face, as well as Wosenee and the rest of the children. For the first time. What a moment! Not a dry eye for miles around. All the neighbors had come over. Singing, dancing, smiling, celebrating, embracing, and joy were in the air for hours and hours. All of us got to meet everyone as well. We saw the house Donna built and the old thatched-roofed shack next to it. We saw the corral and the animals. We saw the letters that had been exchanged through the years and gifts that were given to the family through Donna's generosity. And we saw the light switch that enables those children to do their homework at night. We saw it all, including a smile on Donna's face that was worth a million bucks.

What is it in a person that makes her do what Donna is doing for that family? I believe a lot of it is the assurance Donna feels in her relationship with the Lord. Colossians 1:27 says: "This is the secret: Christ lives in you. This gives you assurance of sharing his glory" (NLT). Her faith is so strong; she's capable of giving that glory away without meeting the person she's giving it to. For years she's trusted the Lord, believing her giving was the right thing for the Bedadas, although she had not met them. First

Timothy 3:13 says, "Those who have served well gain an excellent standing and great assurance in their faith in Christ Jesus" (NIV). Since she "served well" through the years, the Lord opened the door for Donna to travel to Ethiopia to meet this family and to see the fruit of her love and labor. I think we can easily say, Donna has gained an excellent standing in her faith. If we want something to be done, we must do something ourselves: one thing. One little thing that starts the ball rolling. Donna saw that picture of Senayit, and her face was the catalyst for what has saved this family, humanly speaking. Donna has been the tool in God's hand to make all the difference. With her courage and assurance, she's bringing hope to the Bedadas and their surrounding neighbors.

It reminds me of Mark 6 when Jesus sent out the twelve disciples and said to them, "Don't think you need a lot of extra equipment for this. *You* are the equipment"(MSG). That's Donna. She's the equipment God is using to change the face of that girl, that family, that village, and perhaps, that nation.

2

Laying Down the Dream

. . . .

Mandisa

I get asked the same questions pretty often. "Is Simon Cowell that mean in real life?" "What was it like to sing with TobyMac?" "Is Beth Moore as wonderful as she appears to be?" "How tall is Ryan Seacrest?"

It would be wrong of me to throw all of those questions out without giving you the answers, right? Okay. Here we go: I signed a nonfraternization agreement, so apart from the show, I don't know him. Amazing—I got an automatic cool factor just by association. Yes, she's the godliest woman I've ever known. And, not very.

I must admit, I hear certain questions so often that I sometimes go into autopilot when answering. But one question that I get asked pretty regularly makes me pause to consider the implications of my answer.

"How can I become a famous singer like you?"

On the surface, that question seems harmless enough.

I could absentmindedly rattle off, "Dream big and work hard!" which is a perfectly acceptable answer in today's society that relishes the American Dream. But based on my personal experience, I think that question deserves a better response than that.

For as long as I can remember, I have wanted to be a famous singer. As a little girl, I would lock myself in the bathroom, slide in my Whitney Houston cassette tapes (yes, I'm old), and pretend to be a superstar before thousands of adoring fans. My curling iron served as my microphone because, in my opinion, a good microphone needed a cord. Who could know that cordless mics would soon take over the world? Guess I should have used that hairbrush after all! I would wrap a towel on my head because everyone knows that pop stars have long, flowing locks. My kinky, black, shoulder-length hair would never do. I wanted to look like Whitney in her "I Wanna Dance with Somebody" video, with a long, curly, blonde weave cascading down her back. So of course, a beige towel propped up on my head would do the trick.

But I didn't have Whitney's body. Her perfectly toned figure showing through that purple miniskirt was something I couldn't imitate, so I would promise myself that I'd begin the latest fad diet on Monday, which is when every good diet must begin. A liquid-only regime, cabbage soup, or grapefruit fast would do the trick—for at least three days (but that's another story). For the time being, I'd just pretend to be a perfect size 2 for the sake of recreating Miss Houston's video. Music buzzing, mic in hand, the look completed, I would fill the tiny lavatory with the best Whitney Houston impersonation you've ever heard. Alas, after several hours of putting up with the constant roar in the room behind her, my mom would bang on the wall, indicating that the show was over. I would take the hint and sulk to my room, denying my imaginary adoring fans the encore they were demanding.

My mom was the only real-life audience member who was party to my concert enactments. She picked up the cues and encouraged me to join the school choir to hone my craft. There, I learned about blending with others, dynamics, and expression. Eventually I began leading songs in high school, auditioning for honor choirs, and performing solos for community events. When people began paying me just to sing two or three songs at their function, I knew I was on my way! Twenty-five dollars was a lot to a teenager with no job back in the day.

Whenever adults would ask me what I wanted to be when I grew up, I would always reply with, "A singer." In my teen years, people began tagging on the follow-up question, "What will you fall back on?" I would confidently respond with, "I'm not gonna fall back!"

I carried that sentiment with me all the way through college, where I graduated with a bachelor of music degree in vocal performance. It was only after my commencement that my assurance began to waver. As part of the world-renowned Fisk Jubilee Singers, I had sung on stages all across the country and abroad: the Vatican, Macy's Thanksgiving Day Parade, even the United Nations. Attending college in Nashville afforded me the opportunity to perform background for country artists like Shania Twain, Trisha Yearwood, and Faith Hill. I just knew that one of those opportunities would be my big break. But as I crossed the platform to accept my degree in May of 2000, I knew I was crossing a threshold. For the first time in my life, I was out of school. Unlike my fellow graduates, I didn't have law school, graduate school, or an entry-level position waiting for me. I had a degree in vocal performance. That didn't really pave the way for a whole lot of job openings.

My relationship with God had grown by leaps and bounds in college, so I did what I had been doing for the last four years since leaving my California home. I prayed. And when I say I prayed, I'm not talking about short, mellow conversations with the Father. I was on my face, crying out, and pleading for my Creator's guidance. But after several months of crashing on couches and guest rooms of friends and family, I laid my dream of being a famous singer down at the feet of Jesus. Perhaps a little dejected, but mostly desperate, I got to the point where I wanted God's plan for my life more than I wanted my own. I recognized that the safest place for me was in the will of God. Still, if it wasn't singing, I needed God to show me what it was.

I'll never forget how he got my attention. At the suggestion of a friend, I was working my way through a Bible study called *Experiencing God: Knowing and Doing the Will of God* by Henry and Richard Blackaby and Claude King (Nashville: Lifeway, 1990). I was completing that day's lesson, which stated that "God speaks by the Holy Spirit through the Bible, prayer, circumstances, and the church to reveal himself, his purposes, and his ways." I closed the workbook and began talking with God, asking him to speak to me. Several minutes into my prayer time, I glanced down at the workbook, the symbol on the back cover garnering my attention. At first I chalked it up to my wandering mind fighting to focus on an invisible God. But the more I clenched my eyes shut and tried to center my ricocheting thoughts on Jesus, the more that symbol came into view: "LifeWay."

Finally relenting, I confessed to God that I was having a hard time concentrating on him because "LifeWay" kept creeping into my head. Then it was as if the floodgates opened up. It wasn't an audible voice I heard. Just a quiet sense in my spirit that I should look into LifeWay. I immediately moved to the computer and researched more about the Christian bookstore chain, shocked to discover that the corporate offices were located in Nashville. After a few weeks of submitting applications, going in for interviews, and being offered a data entry position in customer service, I obediently followed what I believed to be God's leading.

Admittedly, the thought of typing Sunday school

orders into a computer seemed beneath me. After all, I had just graduated with a college degree. But by now I was near the completion of my *Experiencing God* study. I had finished the chapter that said, "God's invitation for us to work with him always leads to a crisis of belief that requires faith and action." I considered this an act of faith and believed it pleased God. Furthermore, the burden was seemingly on him. I was doing what I felt he said to; now I would walk in trust and allow him to chart my course.

Boy, did he ever! While working at LifeWay, I was introduced to Travis Cottrell, who served as a guest worship leader for a special event LifeWay was holding. I was told that Travis was the worship leader for Beth Moore. While working in customer service, I discovered her LifeWay-sponsored women's events all across the country and never imagined that one day I would be a part of those conferences. But through a series of events orchestrated by the Lord, on July 13, 2001, in Charlotte, North Carolina, I stepped onto a stage in front of fourteen thousand women as part of Beth Moore's worship team.

I traveled with Travis and Beth for the next five years. People who saw me as part of the worship team began asking me to come to their events and lead worship. Travis opened up doors for me to be involved with studio work in Nashville. Eventually I could not juggle all of that with my full-time job at LifeWay, so God moved me on from there.

Ultimately, after once again feeling that tug from the

Holy Spirit, I auditioned for *American Idol* in the fall of 2006. My dream of one day being a famous singer was now secondary to the feeling that singing was what I was called to do. I took that calling seriously, witnessing to contestants and staff, sharing forgiveness with Simon Cowell for cruel remarks he made about my weight, and even singing the gospel song "Shackles (Praise You)" on the *American Idol* stage. All of these were things that many feared would lead to my elimination (And several Internet commentaries believe they did.)

But in the end, following the promptings of the Holy Spirit, being obedient to his directives no matter the cost, and trusting him to order my steps has led me to a life that far surpasses my childhood dreams. I have learned that a life that impresses people is a cheap imitation of a life that impacts people.

So when I am asked the question, "How can I become a famous singer like you?" my answer is a thoughtful one. I share my experiences and explain that each step I took is not necessarily a blueprint for everyone. It was the path God prepared for me. The great news is that God has a plan for each of us (Jeremiah 29:11). My promise is that if you seek God's plan above your own and his face even above your dreams, you will run smack-dab into his purpose for you.

"But more than anything else, put God's work first and do what he wants. Then the other things will be yours as well" (Matthew 6:33 CEV).

3

A Year in the Life

············

Patsy Clairmont

on't you love a shiny New Year? New Year's reeks of resolutions; in fact, each year my list emits a certain familiarity—big time. I'm almost certain I've been making the same "commitments" since Opie sat at Aunt Bea's table, scarfing down sweet potato pie before dashing out to use his slingshot. (If you're too young to remember Opie, I rest my case.)

It gets discouraging to think I haven't advanced beyond this paper trail of promises. Every New Year's, I promise myself: "This will be the time . . . I'll lose weight and keep it off. I'll read and study more. I'll be more organized . . . watch less television . . . be less critical." If you're like me, you really mean it, want it, then seldom achieve it beyond February 1. What's that about?

I think there are innate weaknesses that we come pre-packaged with that we won't totally shake until glory. That doesn't mean we should stop making resolutions toward change—nor does it give us license to douse others in our weaknesses—instead, we should own our frailty, confess our sins to one another, and determine to make an effort in a forward motion.

That's not limited to January, you know. You can begin anew anytime.

What will you resolve in your new year (whenever it begins)?

Next comes spring. For years I lived in Michigan, which means you could get your springtime hopes blurred in a snow squall. I might catch glimpses of robins cavorting about hither and yon (always a good sign), but they were likely only cavorting to avoid shivering. It's not just what I see that fans my expectations; it's also what I smell: soft soil, a faint floral fragrance, and raindrops.

Spring convinces me I need to intentionally lean into life. I need the fresh sap and supple energy spring offers. My days have collected like last year's dry leaves on my porch, turning into years—and how fortunate I am to be able to witness tulips press through hardship, forsythia burst into yellow joy, and watch a parade of tipsy ducklings paddle their way through the murky pond.

How will you celebrate spring?

Summer is layered in moods and demands. She sits in your lap and hugs the air from your lungs like a child who's been pampered far too long. She's lush and fragrant, and the birds never tire of singing praises.

Oh, listen. Can you hear it? The tiny rhythms of the bee darting among the flowers and dipping into sweetness. The working buzz firmly in place alerts us to her presence and reminds us of her purpose. I love her gaudy frock, so unexpectedly tailored.

I love the soft sounds of our flag moving in the stir of a breeze. And the way the daylilies curtsey when the breeze moves through the landscape, as though nodding their approval. The garden chimes get caught up in a whirl of excitement when an unexpected breath of an afternoon storm rushes in. Soon the bass rumbling of thunder will quiet the birds' serenade and cause the bees to shelter inside buttercups.

Yes, I love the musical mosaic of summer—the distant giggles of playing children, the hum of a lawn mower in a neighbor's yard, the clinking of ice cubes against a frosty mug, and the sound of rain dancing across rooftops.

What do you hear in the summer? (Don't miss the music!)

Autumn is truly invigorating; in fact, it makes me feel like rushing into each day and tackling projects with new gusto.

Of course, I'm not so naive that I don't realize what follows this adrenaline-pumping season. I understand that all this color is a prelude to winter, when all the land will shudder under a blanket of snow. But here's what I've learned: if I take advantage of the shots of exhilaration that fall offers, winter is then easier to step through.

Hmm, now that I think about it, I guess that holds true for the little autumns and winters in our daily lives. If I take advantage of my good days, my high-energy hours, then when my wintry gloom (off days, illness, relational strife) sets in, I seem to make it through less debilitated.

Why, I could even apply that seasonal perspective hour by hour. I mean, I have some hours that offer me more accomplishing-strength than others—don't you? Some hours I have more schedule-freedom to get things done— if I don't fritter that time away with distractions. (I confess I'm easily distracted if I'm not vigilant.) I've noted that I have a personal ebb and flow of motivation throughout the day that—if I'm wise—I can take advantage of.

Take morning. Not my most productive hours. But check back with me a little later, and I'll be darting like a deer through a cornfield. So I try not to overwhelm myself with too many to-do lists too early, lest I give up and take refuge behind a haystack with a good book.

What needs to be done in your autumn?

My hometown shines at holiday time. You can count on a snow globe of white stuff dusting rooftops and tree branches like a Currier and Ives card. Les and I loved on a wintry day boot scootin' down Main Street in our Charles Dickens wannabe of a town. Music drifted through the air, confirming that "it's beginning to look a lot like Christmas, everywhere we go . . ." Covered carriages with holly-adorned horses await passengers. In the center of town is a mill pond with a network of "tridges" (bridges with attitude) that allow you to walk on water—or in this case, ice—as you make your way around a winter wonderland of ducks, geese, and Christmas glitter. A gazebo and benches are available for the stouthearted. I prefer to duck into the coffee shop and wrap my hands around a chubby cup of cocoa.

Yep, I love this season of bulky sweaters and fuzzy mittens . . . but not enough that I want it to stay all winter, all the time. Just enough to fill my holiday tank.

It's easy to get caught up in the nostalgia of the holidays (if not the materialism) and neglect the heart of the matter. It's not about gifts, but the Gift-giver. It's not about the lights, but the inextinguishable brilliance of Christ. It's not about the nostalgia, but our current access to the very throne of God because of Christ's entry into our world. Talk about "gift"—we'll be unwrapping that one until glory.

How will you observe the holidays?

And before you know it (how did we get here so fast?), we're back at the starting gate of a brand spanking New Year. We could skip the resolutions this time and just cast ourselves headlong into the new calendar, or we can choose once again to take the higher road. I think there's a reason we feel willing, year after year, to try again—and I don't think it has to do with our own goodness. It's God's generosity that says, "I understand your weaknesses, and

I'm not looking for perfection. I'm looking for a heart that never stops seeking me."

Will you keep seeking, no matter what season you're in? I'm planning to.

"Ask, and God will give to you. Search, and you will find. Knock, and the door will open for you. Yes, everyone who asks will receive. Everyone who searches will find. And everyone who knocks will have the door opened" (Matthew 7:7–8 NCV).

4

Trusting God in All My Ways

....

Lisa Whelchel

The Lord has been talking to me about trust a lot these days. Since I was a little girl, my life verse has been Proverbs 3:5-6, "Trust in the LORD with all your heart and lean not on your own understanding; in all your ways acknowledge him, and he will make your paths straight" (NIV). In my head, I know this to be true, and even in my heart, but it is often difficult for me to walk this out in real life.

Not too long ago, during a quiet morning with God and my Bible and my coffee, I dared to look deep down inside, where my heart is ailing and my mind is racing, and ask myself where I have the most difficult time trusting God. I thought of one, and then another, and then one more.

The first one was my fear that my children would choose the lure of the world over a life wholly submitted to Jesus. I felt challenged to ask myself what I was most afraid of and what would happen if God didn't spare me from that fear. Would I trust him to take care of us all in the midst of the heartache and regret? Oddly enough, I have a deep peace about my children's choosing to serve the Lord with their lives, even if they have to find their own way through some side roads of mistakes and missteps along the way. That's not where the fear shows up because I know that some of the deepest lessons I've learned in my own walk with the Lord come when I've chosen my own way, rather than the path he has prepared for me. It is when he has rescued me from the pit or found me when I am lost that I understand his love the most.

I hate to admit this, but I realized my fear has more to do with what other people would think. Having written books on child rearing, I'm afraid that if my children stray, people would be able to say, "See, that stuff Lisa has been teaching doesn't really work after all." Deep down inside, I am afraid of both being raked over the media coals and also tarnishing God's name.

Another area is my lifetime struggle with weight. Again, upon honest reflection, I discovered that I think I would be okay being a bit frumpy if it were just me as the wife of Steve, who loves me regardless. And my kids already know I'm frumpy from the inside-out. The deeper distrust lies in the fact that I feel like my weight might be distracting to the people I have the privilege of ministering to, who come expecting to see Blair, the television character I played on *The Facts of Life*. Again, I sometimes believe that, by being overweight, I am not being a good steward of the platform God has given me. Plus, I really want to wear great outfits and feel good about myself in them.

Last, I realized I was struggling with the size, significance, and "success" of my ministry. Yes, that is completely unspiritual, self-centered, prideful, and ugly, but I was getting honest, and this dross floated to the top. I often battle feeling like my ministry is not as deep as a real Bible teacher's ministry. I feel like I'm a storyteller and an encourager, but that seems so shallow up next to, say, Anne Graham Lotz or Kay Arthur or . . .

I know it isn't about me or the size of the audience or sales of my books. It is about being the part of the body of Christ that God has created me to be. I know that, but I want more. I want God to be proud of me. And I don't want to disappoint my publishers and event teams and women's ministry directors.

In the quiet of my morning and heart, I bowed my head and asked God to reveal to me the root of these distrust issues. All of a sudden, the tears started to pour. It dawned on me what these three things had in common. There were two threads—wanting to please man and not wanting to disappoint God.

Not that old thing again! I thought I had already dealt with that problem. I've known for years that I struggle with being a people-pleaser, but God has brought instances of dramatic change and years of ongoing healing in the area. I really thought it was taken care of. Apparently not. I was reminded of something I heard a Bible teacher say once, "How would you live if you truly trusted God?"

Well, in regard to my teenage children, I wrote them each a letter and asked them to forgive me for not trusting their own personal relationships with God. Other than some nonnegotiables required to live in our home, I was going to trust them to make good choices, and when they made mistakes, I would trust them to learn from those mistakes and experience, firsthand, God's mercy and grace. If I truly hand them over to God, then God won't be disappointed in me for not being a perfect mother, and it is up to him to worry about everyone else's opinion of me and my children.

Now, about my weight. The truth is, I've made some choices and I'm choosing to not second-guess them. Because of a foot injury, I can't jog, walk, run, or play racquetball like I used to. I could go to the gym and get on the elliptical machine, but I just don't want to give that amount of time, and we don't have the room or the money to buy one for the house. Now that my kids are older, I have the luxury of spending a bit more time in the morning with the Lord than when they were little. I could give part of that up to go to the gym, but I'm not willing to. God loves me the way I am, and if he wants me to lose some weight, then in my weakness he can make me strong. I am willing to work at it, but I just don't have the willpower on my own unless he gives it to me.

The most peaceful work happened in the area of my ministry. I figure there is a need for all measures of warfare in a battle. You need the infantry, the mid-range missiles, and the bomber pilots. I believe wholeheartedly in the men and women on the ground. A huge part of my passion is convincing women that we each have a ministry and we need not look any further than our own families, neighborhoods, and churches to find opportunities to make an eternal difference in the kingdom.

Sure, I would love to be a "bomber pilot" for God and see the power of God explode across the world. But if God wants me to be a mid-range missile and keep my focus on ministering to women with practical encouragement, then I'm not only going to be content; I'm going to thank him for that gift.

I've been a pleaser since childhood. I needed to come face-to-face once again with the mercy of Jesus and let his unconditional love heal me on an even deeper level than before. It is not now, and never has been, about my being a good-enough mother, attractive woman, or powerful minister. My heavenly Father loves and adores me because I'm his little girl. And I please him most when I simply trust him.

5

The Right Road

. . . .

Mary Graham

*I*t may take a long time after meeting someone to realize that person's going to be one of the most influential
people in your life. It's only as I look back forty years that
I realize that when I met Dr. Bill Bright, the founder and
president of Campus Crusade for Christ, it was probably
the most pivotal meeting of my life.

I was finishing a year of graduate school in California
and interviewing for various teaching positions. I'd been
student teaching all year and loved it. I've never liked big
changes, so I had decided to take a job close to home,
continue to be involved with the same friends I'd known
through college, and work in an elementary school in the
neighborhood. I could see it all clearly in my mind's eye. It
seemed safe, easy, and I felt satisfied with my plan.

Then it happened. It was Sunday afternoon of my last
week of student teaching. I was helping a friend with a

reception she was giving for Dr. and Mrs. Bright. While carrying a tray of hors d'oeuvres, I had that life-changing encounter. Dr. Bright, who was there to meet dignitaries, greeted me as he helped himself to something on the tray. He asked my name, how I happened to be there, and then visited just briefly. "It's so nice to meet you. What do you do?" I told him I was about to finish a year of graduate school. "And then what?" he asked. I said, "I'm interviewing for a teaching position."

I remember it as clearly as if it were this morning. That dear man looked me square in the eye and said with all the confidence in the world, "Why don't you come to Arrowhead Springs [then the international headquarters of Campus Crusade for Christ] and let God change your mind?" The question pierced my heart like an arrow. I don't think I said another word. I couldn't get Dr. Bright's question out of my head. I asked myself, "What if God has a plan for my life? What if his plan is different from mine?" The next day, the principal of the school where I was student teaching asked what my plans were because, he said, he'd like to request me for his school. Bill Bright's question came immediately to mind. I hemmed and hawed for a few seconds; then Mr. Maas said to me, "What is it? What are you thinking?" In the end, he encouraged me to go be an "adventurer" for a couple years; then he'd give me a job and I could settle down and have a family. Interestingly, I've not seen him since that day so long ago, but I know—I absolutely know—God used that conversation for me to be more courageous about what Dr. Bright had challenged me to do.

I went to Arrowhead Springs that summer. There God changed my mind, my plans, and my life. Bill Bright became a powerful influence in my life from then on. I often worked with him on special projects and watched as he would get ideas that were so huge and impossible they seemed laughable. But he had such belief, it was hard to doubt him. He taught me nothing is impossible with God.

In the mid-1990s, it was Dr. Bright who listened carefully to the words of Luci Swindoll when she told him about this new Women of Faith ministry and what she was doing in the group. Quite honestly, at the time I considered the vision all but unbelievable—that millions of women of all ages would gather in sports arenas to hear messages from God's Word in an environment of laughter, wonderful music, inspiring stories, and heartfelt camaraderie. Talk about a big idea!

I remember Dr. Bright listening very attentively to Luci. After she finished her story, she said, "We want Mary to come help us." Dr. Bright's response was immediate. He turned to me and said, "Mary, why don't you do it?" I'm sure I looked at him as if to say, "Huh?" And he continued, "I've learned that if God is working someplace as it certainly seems he is here, that's where we need to go." I remember saying, "Even though it's not Campus

Crusade?" And his answer: "You know that doesn't matter, Mary. Why would that matter?"

And so, here I am. God first led Luci to invite me to help, then Dr. Bright to encourage, then me to be willing. My heart was opening to something far beyond my wildest imagination. I couldn't see where the path would lead, but I had confidence in taking the next step. God has his way of going before us, coming behind us, and leading through us. He can make the crooked places straight. That's what he has promised, and that's what he does. We can be assured of that.

Through Bill Bright, I learned that God can do anything. I learned first from him that God loves the whole world and that until we step into eternity, God will use us to talk about his love here, there, and everywhere. Even in huge sports arenas. I learned from Dr. Bright that God loves me, has a wonderful and unique place in this world for me, and will do anything to help me understand that so I don't miss it. And Dr. Bright believed that for everyone on the face of the earth, certainly not just me.

I often say I don't really know how God leads, but I think, at least in my life, he led Bill Bright to push me. And every time that happened, God gave me his assurance that "This is the way . . . walk in it."

As a young girl growing up in a large family in the world's smallest community, it never once occurred to me that God loved me. And I could never have dreamed that he had something in mind for me to know, be, and do. Even after I understood his love for me and his amazing grace, I found it almost unimaginable that he had a plan for my life and a far better one actually than I could have ever dreamed. I'm amazed he used circumstances, personal desires, and gifting, as well as godly men and women, to show me God's perfect will for me. Even though I've never actually heard him say, "Do this, Mary . . . walk this way . . . " I've read in Isaiah 30:21, "This is the right road. Walk down this road" (MSG), and that's what I'm doing. I have complete peace that God has placed me where I am, and he walks with me day by day.

And know this: what he's done for me, he will certainly do for you. He will do it for anyone. Learn to be attentive to the people around you. They may be the very ones God is using in your life. It might be your parents, your boss, or your children. It might be your friends or even your enemies. It might be your circumstances. But in everything, you can rest assured God has your best interests at heart. That's what he wants for his children.

Sometimes we stand in our own way because we're afraid to trust, to move ahead, to believe there is more out there than what we've dreamed. Because we can't see the future, we want to stand still. We feel powerless. But, the truth is, nobody who has a relationship with God is powerless. Hebrews 11:1 tells us, "Faith is the confidence that what we hope for will actually happen; it gives us assurance about things we cannot see" (NLT). So, not only are we given the power to step out of our comfort zone, we're also given the assurance to believe everything will work out.

6

A Sure Thing

....

Lisa Harper

$\mathcal{M}$y friend Jane is basically the poster child of how America's economic downturn has negatively affected so many people. But she's also one of my heroes because of her unwavering confidence in God's faithfulness. Her husband, Wayne, is a mortgage broker, so his income has been steadily declining for several years. At first he and Jane simply tightened their belts, assuming they could ride out the real estate slump. They stopped going out to eat, they started carpooling, Jane made homemade Christmas gifts, and they taught their kids that the latest iPods are not a basic necessity.

When Wayne's commission checks continued to shrivel and become even less regular, they realized more sacrifices would have to be made in order to stay afloat financially. So they pulled their kids out of their beloved Christian academy, enrolled them in public schools, and

Jane—who had stopped teaching to become a stay-at-home mom after their third child was born—got a job. She didn't want to give up the golden hours after school when her kids sat at the kitchen table and narrated the events of their day to her while eating chocolate chip cookies. She didn't want to miss out on their field trips and homeroom parties or race to the ball field from work only to find out her baby hit a triple in the previous inning. But she didn't really have a choice, and I never heard her complain.

A year later, when Wayne's income had dried to a trickle, Jane's company downsized, and she was laid off. Right after finding out, she had to have a complete hysterectomy. Soon, the only way they could pay their mortgage and put food on the table was to take money out of their meager retirement account. Of course, they sent out hundreds of résumés and went to countless networking meetings, but neither was able to find a decent job. Ultimately they had to swallow their pride and ask their church for some financial help. And then the literal rain came. More than thirteen inches of rain in two days.

Like most of us in Middle Tennessee, Jane wasn't initially worried that soggy Saturday in May 2010. That is, until the river running behind their neighborhood surged over its banks. Until water filled up the field across from their house, sloshed across their street, and began seeping into their garage. Then they began putting everything on the floor on top of tables and beds. However, within minutes, the water in their garage had risen several feet, so they hurriedly grabbed some clothes, flipped the main breaker switch, and stepped into rising, muddy floodwaters up to their waists.

Jane said wading toward higher ground while holding a change of clothes in a plastic bag was absolutely surreal. When they were trudging along next to their wide-eyed neighbors, she felt like they were in a scene from a movie. Especially when a big National Guard truck rolled through, causing a wave to tag along behind it like a boat wake, with soldiers in the back encouraging everyone to evacuate. She described how incredibly grateful she was that her family had gotten out safely, but how she couldn't help praying, "God, please . . . please protect our home." She just wasn't sure she could handle losing that too.

They spent the night at a friend's house, and she slept fitfully, waking up often and wondering if their home was completely destroyed or if she'd be able to recover their wedding pictures or the kids' special mementos or her dad's watch. Finally dawn came, and with it came news reports that the river had crested and wasn't expected to rise anymore. Soon afterward, she found out the flood-water had filled their garage to within half an inch of their main floor and then miraculously stopped. The width of a thumbnail was all that stood between them and a total disaster.

Jane and her family literally lived a page out of Isaiah's

prophecy: "He says, 'Don't be afraid, because I have saved you. I have called you by name, and you are mine. When you pass through the waters, I will be with you. When you cross rivers, you will not drown'" (Isaiah 43:1–2 NCV).

And God continues to rescue their family in tangible ways because this week, exactly three months after the flood, both she and Wayne started new jobs. Getting to walk alongside them these past few years has reminded me of how *attentive* our Redeemer is to our requests, which was King David's point when he sang, "The LORD hears good people when they cry out to him, and he saves them from all their troubles" (Psalm 34:17 NCV).

No matter what's going on in our lives—whether we're rolling in the dough or pinching pennies, whether our home is on a hilltop or situated next to a rain-swollen river, whether we're in our fat pants or skinny jeans, whether we're filling in all our Bible study blanks or thinking bad words in traffic—we can be assured of the fact that our heavenly Father is paying attention to us. He is neither deaf nor otherwise preoccupied. He inclines his ear to us and even knows every word we're going to say before it tumbles out of our mouths. God is totally tuned in to our frequency.

Jane's story is also a powerful reminder of God's *accessibility*. Even in her most desperate hours, she sensed his presence. He was right next to her when she lost her job, when she worried about how they would pay the electric bill, and when she shoved some clothes into a Kroger bag, gathered her children to her side, and waded out of her neighborhood. During the darkest night of her soul, the night-light of her heavenly Father's company never flickered or grew dim. This is the theme of a parable Jesus taught in Luke's account:

> Then Jesus said to them, "Suppose one of you went to your friend's house at midnight and said to him, 'Friend, loan me three loaves of bread. A friend of mine has come into town to visit me, but I have nothing for him to eat.' Your friend inside the house answers, 'Don't bother me! The door is already locked, and my children and I are in bed. I cannot get up and give you anything.' I tell you, if friendship is not enough to make him get up to give you the bread, your boldness will make him get up and give you whatever you need. So I tell you, ask, and God will give to you. Search, and you will find. Knock, and the door will open for you. Yes, everyone who asks will receive. The one who searches will find. And everyone who knocks will have the door opened. If your children ask for a fish, which of you would give them a snake instead? Or, if your children ask for an egg, would you give them a scorpion? Even though you are bad, you know how to give good things to your children. How much more your heavenly Father

will give the Holy Spirit to those who ask him!"
(11:5–13 NCV)

Preachers and Sunday school teachers sometimes focus on the neighbor's persistence in this passage and emphasize how we need to be just as relentless in our prayer life. I prefer to look at it from a different vantage point. The Alpha and Omega isn't a supernatural sleepyhead who's reluctant to rouse himself and answer the door. No, the true treasure in this divine tale is the nearness of the children to their father. He's so close he can hear their slightest murmur. They don't have to scream or beg or pound on the door to make him hear them. Even more so than a doting parent lying down next to a child who's having trouble sleeping, is the proximity our Abba Father allows us to enjoy with him.

Even though we cannot yet see God with our eyes, we can rest assured that he is in our immediate midst. He is not some faraway, dispassionate dictator peering down from heaven with a furrowed brow; he is an up close and personal Redeemer, who is in this very moment nearer to us than we can possibly imagine.

And you can take that to the bank!

7

You Are Loved

....

Sheila Walsh

When a Samaritan woman came to draw water, Jesus said
to her, "Will you give me a drink?" . . . The Samaritan
woman said to him, "You are a Jew and I am a Samaritan
woman. How can you ask me for a drink?" . . . Jesus
answered her, "If you knew the gift of God and who it is
that asks you for a drink, you would have asked him and
he would have given you living water."

—John 4:7–10 (NIV)

When I lived in Nashville in the late 1990s, I was a
frequent shopper, so to speak, at the humane society.
I would stop by a couple of times a week and donate supplies, take a look at all the pets, and check on which ones
had been adopted. Every now and then, if there was a particularly challenged animal, malnourished or with a coat

in a bad way, I would take it home and nurse it until it became more adoptable.

There was one cat, Max, that especially drew my attention. One cold night, Max had crawled under the hood of a car and onto the still-warm engine. When the owner of the car started up the engine the next morning, he heard the loud cry as Max's back received an awful wound, about six inches long. The owner of the car was kind enough to bring Max to the shelter, and the vet did what he could, but Max was a sorry sight. He had no fur left on his back, and the fur he did have on the rest of his body was odd, to say the least. It was as if his hair had all decided that it was free rein on how-to-grow-cat-hair-day and seemed to point in at least a dozen directions.

"What breed of cat is Max?" I asked one day.

"I don't think Max has any particularly dominating breed," the girl cleaning out the cages said. "I'm not sure how we'll ever get him adopted. He's a bit of everything!"

So, of course, I took Max home that day.

He was one of the sweetest animals I have ever had the joy of loving. It seemed to me that his devotion came because someone saw beyond his wounds to his wonderful heart. He rewarded that love with warmth and was the gentlest animal I have ever known. He also had quite an unusual meow. The vet thought it likely that his vocal cords had been crushed in the accident, but I loved the sound; it gave Max a songlike meow. As I think about Max now, I think the love I showed him is what we all long for really, don't you? We all want someone to see beyond the scars and bumps and bruises of life to who we really are inside.

That is the whole heart of the gospel. Jesus sees beyond what others see to a woman or a man or child who is worth loving, worth dying for. We can trace it through the entire canon of Scripture. Story after story tells us about the way God in Christ broke through social stigma, disease, and disappointment to transform hearts one by one with his love. Perhaps that is what is most striking to me about Christ's encounter with the Samaritan woman at the well: Christ saw beyond her culture, her gender, and her string of broken relationships that she wore like a scarlet letter. Christ saw a woman who was worth dying for and that would bind her heart to his, all her heart. That love turned her from an outcast into an evangelist. God's love always sees beyond the impossible to what is possible in his hands. His love invites us in.

One of my favorite chapters in the whole Bible is Romans 8. It is an almost perfect theology in itself. It begins with no condemnation:

> Therefore, there is now no condemnation for those who are in Christ Jesus, because through Christ Jesus the law of the Spirit of life set me free from the law of sin and death. (Romans 8:1–2 NIV)

It ends with no separation:

> Who shall separate us from the love of Christ? Shall trouble or hardship or persecution or famine or nakedness or danger or sword? As it is written: "For your sake we face death all day long; we are considered as sheep to be slaughtered." No, in all these things we are more than conquerors through him who loved us. For I am convinced that neither death nor life, neither angels nor demons, neither the present nor the future, nor any powers, neither height nor depth, nor anything else in all creation, will be able to separate us from the love of God that is in Christ Jesus our Lord. (Romans 8:35–39 NIV)

Have you ever read those verses out loud? I highly recommend it. It's impossible to read them, I think, without being deeply moved. So why is it that we sometimes lack the assurance that there is nothing that can separate us from God's love? Why do we doubt that, as we are right now, we are worth loving? I sometimes wonder if it is easier for a woman who has totally lost her way to accept the love of God than a woman who has simply lost heart in the middle of the journey. If we have really messed up in a way that is not only known to us but to others, we are acutely aware that we stand in need of the grace, mercy, and forgiveness of God. But if we move from day to day doing our best to take care of our family and our home, we can get a little lost in the shuffle.

Here is the truth, as I understand it from God's Word. Just as you are right now, you are totally loved by our Father. There is nothing you did to earn it. There is nothing you can do to change it. All we can do is run to it and allow our Father to embrace us.

If you have ever felt like a stray or one who wears a scarlet letter or just a woman who feels as if she does the same thing over and over again—don't be surprised when God's love takes you in:

> *This is a dream I have*
> *That there might be a place*
> *Where before I cross the threshold*
> *They recognize my face*
>
> . . . . . .
>
> *You belong here*
> *Welcome home!*
>
> —*"You Belong Here"*
> by Chris Eaton and Kyle Matthews, 2003

8

Beginning, Middle, End

．．．．．．．．．．．

Marilyn Meberg

There is a beginning, a middle, and an end to every-thing on this earth. One of my most unfavorite ends is the completion of a fudgy creation called chocolate vol-cano pudding cake. At the beginning of this gastronomical treat, I am filled with happy anticipation. At the beginning of my consumption, I don't think about the reality that it will soon come to an end. It's too early to think about it, but somewhere in the middle of this treat, I become aware I am nearing the end; I will have to put my fork down.

Some endings fill us with sadness or regret while other endings fill us with relief. In all cases, however, "the end is in sight." One of the endings that filled me with relief was knowing my home economics sewing class would ultimately end. Although that horrendous experi-ence was more than fifty years ago, I well remember the three stages of beginning, middle, and end. I began the class with total optimism, certain I would ultimately learn to sew my own clothes.

By the middle of the sewing semester, I became acutely aware that the relationship with my sewing machine was totally adversarial. For example, I did not understand the intricacies of threading the needle. (Remember this was years ago when the earth's crust was still cooling. I have no idea about the needle-and-thread relationship in this era.) Not understanding the inner workings of my machine and consequently lagging behind, I valiantly tried and failed to finish my projects on time. The final and most pitiful experience that caused me to long for the coming "end" was when I unwittingly sewed my project into the skirt I was wearing. This tragic story is given in more painful detail in my first book, *Choosing the Amusing*. My point here is that I was relieved beyond measure when I experienced the end of my sewing class. Even now, centuries later, the sight of a sewing needle causes me to hyperventilate.

But what I want to focus on here is this: we may be more emotionally equipped to walk through the beginning and middle phases of our experiences, but sometimes the end phase is our most challenging. When that phase does not provide relief, but instead brings sadness or grief, how might we deal with that phase? Should we fight against it, go into denial, or sink into a little heap, saying, "Whatever"? I say fight it! It's true: endings are inevitable, but we don't always know the timetable for the inevitable.

Maybe it makes sense to fight against it until . . . well . . . the end.

With my husband's cancer diagnosis came the words, "You have four to six months to live," the medical prediction for Ken's end. He decided to fight it. He received chemo and radiation, and he radically altered his diet. Instead of four months, he lived fourteen months. In those months, we witnessed both of our kids receiving engagement rings, heard their plans for marriage, and took a family vacation. Only God knows the divine timetable; until the moment when God says, "Okay, honey . . . now," we have the option to fight against the inevitable.

Sometimes the "end" is not about physical death but about the end of life as we've known it. There, too, we decide whether to fight or give in. Yesterday I was in tears as I watched a young man who had lost both legs from a rocket-propelled grenade in the war in Afghanistan. In a television interview, he looked straight into the camera and said, "Never give up." Then, on personally designed artificial legs, he stepped up to his golf ball, swung, and sent it flying beautifully down the fairway, where it landed only ten feet from the cup on the green. The camera followed him as he sank the shot in one stroke. At the beginning of this young man's experience of double amputation, he had no hope of ever walking again. But he fought. Yesterday I watched him play golf.

There is yet another end phase we hear about

frequently, and that is the potential end of this planet based on humanity's disregard for proper "earth-care." Every time I drink bottled water from a plastic bottle and then realize how toxic those non-biodegradable bottles are to our landfills, I feel guilty. Some of us have possibly become immune to the dire reports we hear about our contribution to pollution. However, I recently read a report that jerked me to attention. We are facing a weird but decidedly serious menace: jellyfish! What?

In 1999, not far from Manila, forty million people were abruptly plunged into darkness; the lights were not restored for nearly twenty-four hours. What happened? A gigantic influx of jellyfish was sucked into the cooling pipes of a coal-fired power plant. More than fifty dump trucks were filled with jellyfish and removed from the site.

Another jellyfish incident was documented off the coast of Ireland as a swarm of jellyfish stung and asphyxiated more than one hundred thousand farmed salmon off the coast of Ireland. The jellyfish swarm reportedly was thirty-five feet deep and covered ten square miles. There is admittedly a huge "ick" factor with these accounts, but they become more than "ick" when the jellyfish phenomenon is reported to stretch from the fiords of Norway to the resorts of Thailand. By clogging cooling equipment, jellies have shut down nuclear power plants in several countries and partially disabled aircraft carriers. The waters off California's Monterey Bay have millions of jellies, as do other U.S. coastlines. Jellyfish reproduce so rapidly that many scientists expect jellyfish to take dominance in one ecosystem after another. Mercy! This sounds like a sci-fi movie!

You may be asking, "What, Marilyn, do these jellyfish accounts have to do with the discussion about everything on earth having a beginning, a middle, and an end? Did you get a bit sidetracked?"

I have to admit my attention is frequently captured by the quirky and the odd, so the bad behavior of these blobby creatures engaged me immediately. But there is a deeper issue here other than my fascination by the fact that there are fifteen hundred species of jellyfish ranging in size from microscopic to more than seven feet wide and one hundred feet long. And there are archeological digs that suggest they've been around more than a million years!

So okay, here's the deeper issue. Genesis 1:1 states, "In the beginning God created the heavens and the earth" (NIV). Everything and everyone had a perfect beginning. When the Fall occurred, everything then left a great beginning and headed for the often troubling middle and occasionally a disastrously tragic end. In spite of that sobering alteration to our perfect beginnings, God has challenged us to fight against all that will threaten our middle and end phases. That divine challenge applies to our personal life decisions as well as those decisions that affect our planet.

God told Adam he was placed in the garden to serve

and protect it. Scripture reminds us in Psalm 24, that "the earth is the LORD's (KJV)," and we are its temporary care-takers. When the rhythms of creation get out of balance, to the degree we humans can fight to restore that balance, we must do so. That, dear ones, brings me back to the topic of jellyfish. The abundance of jellyfish is thought to be the result of unwise human choice. The fishing indus-try has fished out the creatures that eat jellyfish: primarily red tuna, swordfish, and sea turtles. Since they are no lon-ger there to dine on jellies, the ecosystem has gotten out of balance, and the jellies have gone on an eating binge. What are they eating? The madly multiplying plankton that anchovies usually eat; but the anchovies also are being fished out, so that leaves a sumptuous diet of plankton for the jellies, who eat, burp, and reproduce.

So what are we supposed to do about all this besides keep a wary eye on the water filling our bathtub? I chose jellies as one of the many challenges our earth faces simply because of the compelling "ick" factor. But in all serious-ness, we as a people are called to be wise caretakers of our earth. We can't sit back and say "whatever" as we march to its inevitable end. We must tune in to the many ways we can conserve and preserve our God-given resources until, according to God's timetable, he says "Okay, honey . . . now."

But here's encouraging news. We are approaching a time when there will be no end phase—only perfection beyond imagining that will go on forever. I won't have to calculate how quickly or slowly I eat my chocolate volcano pudding cake. The health and vitality we long for will be fully ours, and they will never end due to accidents or diseases. We will never be assigned tasks we hate and for which we are ill suited. There will be no more pollution or imbalance of our ecosystems. The beauty of nature, with its Eden-like perfection, will be restored. We'll never run out of clean water, fresh air, fresh food, or perfect temperature. Sounds heavenly, doesn't it? And of course, it is.

So with all that in mind, if you find yourself overwhelmed by one of life's cycles, be encouraged. You are making your way out of that cycle and heading for possible earthly relief and for sure heavenly perfection. First Corinthians 2:9 states, "No eye has seen, no ear has heard, and no mind has imagined what God has prepared for those who love him" (NLT). That's one prediction we don't want to fight against!

About the Contributors

. . . .

2011 Women of Faith Speakers

Patsy Clairmont has a quick wit and depth of biblical knowledge that combine in a powerful pint-size package. A recovering agoraphobic with a pronounced funny bone, Patsy speaks to women from all walks of life, giving love and hope as she does. Patsy is the author of multiple books, including her most recent, *Kaleidoscope*.

Mary Graham is president of Thomas Nelson Live Events, a division of Thomas Nelson, Inc., which hosts Women of Faith, America's largest women's conference. Mary serves as host for the conference, works closely with speakers and musicians, directs seventy-five employees, and supervises all phases of the ministry. Prior to joining Women of Faith, Mary was director of international ministries for Insight for Living. She also invested thirty years with Campus Crusade for Christ International.

Lisa Harper definitely brings the Bible to life. Chances are you won't ever look at the Bible the same way again after hearing or reading her fresh take on the Scriptures. Lisa holds a master of theology from Covenant Theological

Seminary. Her multiple books include *Untamed: How the Wild Side of Jesus Frees Us to Live* and *Love with Abandon*.

Mandisa, who traveled on Beth Moore's worship team for five years, was thrust into the spotlight as a finalist on the fifth season of *American Idol*. Since then she has become a Christian recording artist, garnering multiple Grammy and Dove Award nominations. Her chart-topping full-length albums, *True Beauty*, *It's Christmas*, and *Freedom*, will be followed up with her fourth project, releasing April 2011. She is the author of *Idoleyes: My New Perspective on Faith, Fat, and Fame*.

Marilyn Meberg is the author of several books, including *Glimmers of Grace*, *Love Me Never Leave Me*, and *Tell Me Everything*. Never one to avoid the hard questions of life, Marilyn shares the wisdom she has gained from two master's degrees, a career as an English professor at Biola University, and a private counseling practice.

Luci Swindoll is full of anticipation, fun, and a sense of adventure that just won't quit. Her exuberant love for life has seen her through a career as a corporate executive at Mobil Oil, performances with the Dallas Opera, and work as vice president of public relations at her brother Chuck's ministry, Insight for Living. She is the author of many books, including her most recent, *Living Life Differently*.

Sheila Walsh, a former co-host of *The 700 Club*, is author of the award-winning Gigi, God's Little Princess series, *The Shelter of God's Promises*, *Beautiful Things Happen*

When a Woman Trusts God, and a new fiction trilogy, *Angel Song*. She also is a successful recording artist.

Lisa Whelchel, whose first appearance on *The New Mickey Mouse Club* launched her busy acting career, is best known for her role as Blair on the perennial hit TV show *The Facts of Life*. She is the author of *Friendship for Grown-Ups* and *Creative Correction*.

What will your Women of Faith weekend be like?

Are you ready for two days *"filled to the brim with friendships, love, and a connection to God and his Word like never before"*? (That's how Amanda G described her recent Women of Faith event.)

How about the kind of weekend Annette M. said was *"inspiring, uplifting, introspective, heart- and gut-wrenching, soul-cleansing, and over-the-top fantastic!"* Diane C. called Women of Faith, *"The best weekend I've had in a long time."*

What will you say about *your* Women of Faith experience?
You won't know until you go!

> I would encourage all women in all stages of life to attend! Do not miss this wonderful, encouraging weekend! Lisa G.

>> Don't miss this opportunity!
Dates, locations, talent, registration, and more at **womenoffaith.com** or call
888.49.FAITH (888.493.2484).